DATE		

ONE HOUR IN PARIS

ONE HOUR IN PARIS

A True Story of Rape and Recovery

KARYN L. FREEDMAN

The University of Chicago Press *Chicago and London*

KARYN L. FREEDMAN lives in Toronto, Canada,
where she is an associate professor of philosophy
at the University of Guelph.

The University of Chicago Press, Chicago 60637
The University of Chicago Press, Ltd., London
© 2014 by Karyn L. Freedman
All rights reserved. Published 2014.
Printed in the United States of America

23 22 21 20 19 18 17 16 15 14   1 2 3 4 5

ISBN-13: 978-0-226-07370-5 (cloth)
ISBN-13: 978-0-226-11760-7 (e-book)
DOI: 10.7208/chicago/9780226117607.001.0001

Library of Congress Cataloging-in-Publication Data
Freedman, Karyn Lynne, 1968–
One hour in Paris : a true story of rape and recovery /
Karyn L. Freedman.
pages ; cm
ISBN 978-0-226-07370-5 (cloth : alkaline paper)—
ISBN 978-0-226-11760-7 (e-book)
1. Freedman, Karyn Lynne, 1968– 2. Rape victims—
Biography. 3. Women philosophers—Canada—
Biography. I. Title.
B995.F744A3 2014
362.883092—dc23
[B]
2013027389

♾ This paper meets the requirements of ANSI/
NISO Z39.48–1992 (Permanence of Paper).

Contents

Prologue

There are images in my head that do not belong there. No matter how hard I try to get rid of them they will not go away. It is as if they are permanently seared into my brain and written over my body. Over the years I have tried to talk them out, and when that didn't work, I talked louder. I have tried to write them out, paint them out, fight them out, and, by sheer determination, will them out. Occasionally, in darker moments, I have tried to drink them out. These efforts were not futile (except for the drinking). Each one helped in lessening the hold the images have over me, but none was entirely successful. They are mine for life, and that just might be the single most important fact that we can learn about psychological trauma. It is permanent. The psychological damage that results from uncontrollable, terrifying life events is profound. Not everyone who experiences a traumatic event becomes psychologically traumatized, but the ones who do are faced with enduring emotional, cognitive, and physiological consequences. This is true universally, even if the experience and aftermath of trauma varies historically and culturally. It has been over twenty years since I was raped, and I have finally reconciled myself to the immutability of trauma. I now understand that psychological trauma is not something from which one ever fully recovers. It is a chronic condition, and that means that the rape is forever my shadow. It tracks me everywhere. It follows me up the street to my local coffee shop in the middle of the day, and when I come home from a late night out with friends it is just over my shoulder. It is with me at work, in the classroom, and at play, in the dressing room before one of my recreational hockey games. Most especially, it stalks me in the bedroom. Twenty years later and I still have to work to put myself to sleep at night—and sleep is relatively easy, compared to sex. My body is interminably sensitive to the touch, the violence of the rape imprinted all over it—on my breasts, my neck, my lower back, and everything important below that. For the most part I have not let this stop me from having sex, or enjoying it, for that matter, which I know to be a victory of sorts. But like most survivors of sexual violence I am anything but carefree with my body. I am never fully uninhibited when lying naked with another person, and I have had to set up strict boundaries—no touching my head, no dark rooms, no spontaneous moves—in order to protect myself from the images that will otherwise wash over me.

Having said that, the shadow of the rape is less conspicuous today than it once was. That is the result of a decade or so of hard work with an exceptional therapist, work which has shown me that a traumatic experience does not have to be a place of pain forever. With enough time and effort, survivors have a chance of moving through the memory of their experience and making it a place of transformation and emotional growth. My personal experience has taught me that to get out from under the hold of the memory of my rape I first had to live in it. Now, for the most part, I am able to remember the experience without being held hostage by it. Still, when I think about what happened to me in Paris, France, on the night of August 1, 1990, my left shoulder folds forward to protect my neck and my anus muscles shut tight. These bodily ticks are one sort of reminder of that night, and there are a host of others, too. These can make it a challenge to talk about my rape, or write about it for that matter, but nevertheless, I think it is important to do so. Some time ago I made a commitment to myself to tell my story, in part because I am persuaded by the notion that there are some phenomena, some of life's events, that can be best accessed from the inside. I think that sexual violence is one of these. If I have learned anything from my experience as a rape survivor, then perhaps others can learn from my account of it. My hope is that through focusing intimately inward I am able to relate something that others can connect with.

I made the decision to write this book for another reason, too. It is close to fifty years since the beginning of the second wave of the women's movement in North America, which saw a number of seminal publications on the ubiquity of rape, and yet, despite impressive gains on a number of women's issues, sexual violence remains a dirty secret. Through statistics we may know of rape's pervasiveness—one in three women worldwide, one every ten seconds—the social and cultural pressure on women to keep their stories private is, for many, an insurmountable hurdle. As a result, survivors of sexual violence remain anonymous, effectively closeted. This is deeply regrettable. It both reinforces the shame that we struggle against and widens the gap between who we are and how others see us. This also has the unfortunate consequence of making rape look like a personal problem, a random event that happened to me, for instance, because of where I was, what I was wearing, or who I was with, instead of what it really is: an epidemic faced by women and children worldwide which is the manifestation of age-old structural inequalities which persist between men and women. By speaking out about their experiences of sexual violence, survivors can help us to see the problem of rape as a problem of social justice. Thus, bodily tics notwithstanding, I have decided to tell the story of my rape. The story has some twists and turns, but it is a true story from start to finish, though I am likely guilty of some exaggeration and evasion, however inadvertent. For instance, as I remember it, the knife that was pressed into my neck (and other body parts) during the attack was ten inches long with a shallow serrated edge, but at least one reliable record of my experience—the official transcript of the pretrial *indictment*, which contains my deposition—says nothing about whether the knife's edge was serrated. Now, it could be that the edge was serrated but that I failed to mention this fact in my testimony. Or it could be that because the knife felt sharp I drew the conclusion that it had a jagged edge. And I did not have a tape measure handy, so maybe the knife was eight inches long, or twelve. More to the point, I am certain that there are elements of my story that I do not remember, as paradoxical as that may sound. Our minds are powerfully protective of us and can block memories that we lack the emotional resources to handle.

Just over a decade ago, when I began in earnest to deal with the trauma of my rape, I discovered that my dad kept a file of every single correspondence and document related to it. I now call this my "rape file," and it is over two inches thick. It includes the dozens of letters that I received over the years from various representatives of the judicial system in Paris (lawyers, prosecutors, magistrates and clerks), as well as each response that my dad sent back on my behalf from his law firm (both his handwritten drafts and the translations he had done by a bilingual colleague). It also contains medical documents, Visa receipts of airline tickets, and hotel bills from a couple of trips to Paris, a copy of the aforementioned transcript of the pretrial *indictment* from the cour d'appel of Paris, and a copy of the trial *judgment* from the cour d'assises. Some of this stuff I had never seen before, and the rest of it I had not seen for close to a decade. In that time I had told the story of my rape to a handful of close friends and therapists, and when I read through my deposition, my own pretrial testimony, I was shocked to discover that over the years I had blocked from my memory and thus omitted from my retelling of the event a second round of violent penetrations.

No doubt there are other significant facts about the experience that I have erased from memory but which, unfortunately, I cannot handily find out about by reading through my rape file. The ways that our memories infuse content with meaning, conceal meaning from content, or block content altogether can teach us something important about trauma. It can also teach us something about truth, and about freedom. Certainty may be less forthcoming than we might have hoped. But if I am sure

of anything it is that there are innumerable other survivors out there whose experiences mirror mine. If you
are one of these people then you might find certain parts
of what follows triggering, in particular the first chapter,
but please know this: I wrote this book for you.

1: Paris, August 1, 1990

Shortly after noon on Wednesday, August 1, 1990, I boarded a train in Amsterdam that was headed to Paris. I was twenty-two years old. I had just spent four days in Utrecht. Before that I was in Nice for three days, preceded by equally short stints in Florence, Rome, Munich, Budapest, Prague, Warsaw, Krakow, Berlin, Heidelberg, Freiberg and Vienna. I was backpacking through Europe for the summer. I had a Eurail Pass, which covered all of Western Europe and parts of Eastern Europe and which enabled you to board any train in any direction at your whim, so long as there was an empty seat. It was designed for guileless foreigners like me who thought that the best way to get to know Europe was to hop from country to country, and I was making the most of it. It was my first time overseas and it began with considerable promise. In May, my mom, dad, two sisters, and I flew from our home in Winnipeg, Manitoba, via Zurich and Vienna to Israel for a three-week-long family vacation. I had belatedly moved through my teenage years, which were drawn full of angst and rebellion, and for the first time in a long while I was relaxed and easy to be around. By all accounts, it was a great family trip. We had a sagacious Israeli named Michael for a guide, and he took us from one end of the Promised Land to the other, supplementing what I had learned about the country in my youth, courtesy of my private Hebrew school education, and by then mostly long forgotten. Every square mile of Israel was fascinating, from the historic old city of Jerusalem and the Western Wall to the cosmopolitanism of Tel Aviv. We swam suspended in the Dead Sea, climbed Masada, and picked our way through ramshackle Bedouin markets. We spent a quiet afternoon at Yad Vashem, the Holocaust Museum, and had lunch at Yad Mordechai, a *kibbutz* that was renamed in 1943 in honor of Mordechai Anielewicz, the leader of the Warsaw Ghetto Uprising (two months later I stood, awestruck, on Anielewicza Street in Warsaw, where the uprising took place). We skipped the Gaza Strip, which was unsafe even then. I have great pictures from this trip. It was fascinating and edifying, and it was a happy time. We stayed in nice hotels and ate good food and at the end of the three weeks we flew together to Vienna, at which point my mom, dad, and older sister, Jacqueline, returned home. My younger sister, Lisa, and I stayed in Vienna for a couple more days and then began our summer sojourn together. The plan was to travel for a week or so through Germany and then split up to travel with our respective friends for a couple of months before meeting up again in Paris in the second week of August. We were going to spend our last week there together before flying home on August 13. Instead, I left Paris, alone, on the morning of August 2.

My sisters and I have always been very close, and traveling with Lisa was marked by the kind of easiness you can only get with family. Europe was full of small miracles for us. We were endlessly impressed by the architecture of history, and each experience seemed richer than the last. We went to Berlin and stood where the Wall had come down the year before. We toured the Reichstag and naively poked fun at armed guards in East Berlin (who were humorless and impervious to our advances). There were vestiges of the Holocaust throughout Germany—indeed, throughout Europe—memorialized in monuments and museums. I have never been religious, but being Jewish has always been central to my identity, and traveling around Europe felt like a tour through the history of anti-Semitism. The attempted annihilation of the Jewish people became tangible for me for the first time and, seriously impressionable, I started to read Elie Wiesel and Primo Levi. A month later I went to Poland to see Auschwitz and stood, at a loss for understanding, under the *"Arbeit macht frei"* sign at the entrance to the main camp, only to return to Germany for a second time to go to Dachau, the Nazi concentration camp outside of Munich. My immersion in Holocaust literature turned out to be a postrape saving grace, or at least so I thought at the time. It provided me with a clear juxtaposition: although what happened to me was bad, compared to the obscenity of the death camps and the mass extermination of the Jews, well, there was no comparison. What I later came to understand was that this convenient contrast was just one among many intellectual devices I was able to rely on in order to avoid facing the pain of my own traumatic experience.

After Lisa and I split up I spent some time traveling alone and some time traveling with a good friend from Winnipeg. Being on my own was a test that I felt I needed to pass. I had spent the previous couple of years cultivating an image of myself as an independent woman, and although I was occasionally lonely and insecure, I had this idea that if I beat down my anxiety then at least there would be truth in the persona. This would prove to be a recurring theme following my rape, and it wasn't entirely disingenuous. I did gain a robust sense of accomplishment from meeting the challenge of getting by on my own. It was an adventure and, at times, was thrilling. Still, it was a lot easier traveling with a friend. We went to Italy and Germany, but the highlight of our time together was Prague. Nineteen eighty-nine had been the year of the Velvet Revolution, which saw the overthrow of the Communist government in what was then Czechoslovakia, and one year later the country was just opening up to tourists. Prague was the most beautiful city that I had ever seen, and we spent weeks there. Cigarettes were a dime a pack and the view of the Prague Castle from the Charles Bridge was exceptional. Our days were idyllic. We ate waffles from street vendors and warm gusts of summer moved around us.

In early June, while still traveling with Lisa, I spent a day and a half in Heidelberg with my ex-boyfriend who was there for the summer, studying German. I think he now goes by his given name, David, but back then everyone knew him by his nickname, Stream. Stream and I met in 1987 in New York City. I lived there for two years while attending the Fashion Institute of Technology (FIT), where I studied fashion merchandising. I had gotten there by accident. I graduated high school—barely—in 1986. The rebellious years that I referred to earlier were at their peak then and I was struggling to find my way. I went through half a pack of cigarettes a day and spent my weekends smoking pot and getting high. Those were dark days. I would regularly sneak out of my house in the middle of the night to meet other wayward friends and then sleep through classes the following day (during my junior and senior years, my absentee rates were routinely higher than my grades). The only thing I was focused on was avoiding the emotional consequences of my privileged, middle-class, suburban upbringing.

My parents are intelligent, funny, and charismatic people, and they are also kind, loving, and supportive. They have nurtured us into a very close-knit family and I cherish my relationships with them both, but things have not always been smooth. They were the children and grandchildren of immigrants, and the first generation of Jews in Winnipeg not to have significant opportunities closed off to them through anti-Semitism. There was a lot of pressure on them and their contemporaries to become successful professionals and community leaders. They pulled this off with great finesse and today I am humbled by their accomplishments, but when I was growing up I wanted more time and attention from them than their careers permitted. I became an angry child and those feelings dominated my teen years, my rebellion a cover for my insecurities. I came very close to failing high school, and indeed would have were it not for the goodwill of a guidance counselor and a drafting teacher who had confidence in me at a time when I had none in myself. They helped me graduate by letting me run a fashion show for a couple of credits. It is a bit hard to believe now, but it was due to the success of that show that I determined that I had a future in the fashion industry, which is how I ended up in New York City at FIT.

Stream was from upstate New York, the Poughkeepsie area. If I remember correctly, he earned his nickname from being able to traverse successfully myriad difficult mountain trails and rivers and, yes, streams in the vicinity. He was also at FIT, and we were two fish out of water. I had decided pretty quickly after arriving that fashion was not for me. I can't pin down the precise cause or date, but after a couple of months in New York City I had a cerebral awakening of sorts, and I turned from high school dropout to aspiring intellectual. Suddenly, I was itching to study something more academic. (I took my first philosophy course at FIT from an imposing man named Spencer Schein who, as far as I can tell, is still teaching there.) I can't remember what program Stream was in, but he wasn't happy at FIT either. As soon as he got there (or maybe even before that), he decided he wanted to be a writer. He made up his mind to transfer to a good liberal arts university to study creative writing and poetry, which is how, a couple of years later, he ended up at Bard College, a prestigious liberal arts college in upstate New York overlooking the Hudson River. One of Bard's acclaimed faculty members, a poet and literary critic named Édouard Roditi, would eventually become Stream's professor and mentor. Both he and Stream would have fateful roles to play in the story of my rape.

Stream and I met midway through my first year in New York and dated for the next year and a half. I had been in love once before, but this was my first serious relationship and I fell hard. The relationship was full of emotional messiness, which struck me then as romantic but which I now see as a sign of our youthful inexperience. Still, we were truly in love. We spent all our time together and shared what we had to share, and the result was an intensely intimate connection. We stayed up late listening to Joni Mitchell and found ourselves in the dark. In the spring of 1989 I graduated from FIT and moved back to Winnipeg to pursue an undergraduate degree in philosophy at the University of Manitoba, enrolling full-time a couple of months later, in the fall of 1989. Stream and I broke up but remained best of friends. We talked often and wrote each other long letters. He came to visit me in Winnipeg that winter, over the holiday break, and we were together for another three weeks, only to split up again when he left. We agreed that a long-distance relationship was unsustainable but fell quickly back into our old roles when we saw each other in Heidelberg that summer. We were together for only thirty hours, but we had a great time. I was still very much in love with him, and I know this for certain because my journal entries from that summer say so.

I have kept a journal off and on throughout my life, starting in my late teens, and I had taken a fresh one with me to Europe that summer. I now refer to it as my "rape journal." It took me two months to fill the first half of it and close to three years to finish it. My writing was one thing that came to an almost full halt after my rape. I picked up the habit again with resolve in the mid-1990s and continued to write in journals for the next ten years, but none of these other journals exist today. Following the time that I completed my rape journal in January

1993, I destroyed each subsequent journal when I was done writing in it. I simply could not bear to reread them. I had been psychologically crippled by the trauma of the rape and this was transparent in most entries, which centered predominantly on the goings-on of one messed up romantic relationship or another. I could not hide from my own words, which I found exceedingly embarrassing. So once the pages of my journals were full I tore them up into pieces, or I burned them in a garbage can (just in case the message wasn't clear enough). I regret that now. I wish I had been less hard on myself. I could have learned a lot from those journals. The miracle is that I never threw out my rape journal. I now keep it in a Ziploc in a filing cabinet alongside my rape file. It's got a pretty floral-patterned cover, although the binding was never any good and the pages had already started to slip apart back in 1990. But I am very careful with it and though its pages are now well worn, I have not lost a single one. It makes me sad every time I read it. The entries leading up to August 1, 1990 are rich in excitement and anticipation, dripping with self-conscious melancholy and punctuated by regular smoke breaks. The uncertainty of youth is palpable but the overall impression is one of happy innocence. I would never sound quite that way again. The entries dated after August 1 read as hollow and sad, stunted. They are abbreviated; the adventure in my voice is gone.

Though Stream and I spent only a day together in Heidelberg in June, our plan was to meet up again in late July. He had a free place to stay in Paris and I was invited to join him there. We left it up in the air and promised to keep in touch. These were the days before the

Internet and cell phones made communication in and across foreign countries easy. Instead, we had to anticipate where the other one would be and when, and hope that our letters reached each other through the American Express office in some stipulated city. In late June I wrote to him in Heidelberg to tell him that I would be in Budapest at the start of July. On July 2, I celebrated my twenty-second birthday with friends in Prague and the next day I boarded a train to Vienna, where I spent a few more days with friends before taking off on my own to Budapest. Had Budapest been my first stop in Eastern Europe I think I would have appreciated it more. It is a majestic city, but it couldn't compare to the beauty and charm of Prague. I stayed with a family in Old Buda who did not speak a word of English but who were very kind to me — they fed me, and even did my laundry, which, as any backpacker can appreciate, was a godsend. I spent most of my time wandering around the touristy parts of the city, hanging out in coffee shops and writing in my journal. After a few days on my own I met a couple of nice guys from the U.S. who were traveling with a woman from Holland, and the four of us stuck together for the rest of my time there. One day we went to a Stalin exhibit at a museum in town and then later that night, in mock contrast, attended a Pink Floyd light show at an open-air amphitheater. I got along well with the Dutch woman, who generously invited me to visit her in Utrecht later in the month. That turned out to be my final stop before heading to Paris on August 1.

I checked the American Express office in Budapest every day, looking for a letter from Stream. It finally arrived on July 10. He wrote that he had decided to leave

Heidelberg earlier than initially planned so that he could travel around a bit before going to Paris at the end of July. He asked me to meet him in Hamburg before going to Paris, but I decided to delay our reunion and instead I returned to Prague, where I had a brief fling with a cute British guy. I made a couple more stops after that, first in Italy and then the South of France, before visiting my new Dutch friend in Utrecht. I stayed with her for four days, wandering around Utrecht and going on day trips to Amsterdam where, like most of my fellow backpackers, I spent a portion of each day, wide-eyed, hanging out in coffee shops, smoking pot.

*

On Wednesday, August 1, 1990, just after noon, I caught a train at Amsterdam Central Station that was due to arrive in Paris, at Gare du Nord, around 5:30 p.m. I had written to Stream to give him my itinerary and he had replied that he would meet me at the train station. I spent the train ride writing in my journal about how quickly the summer had passed and musing about what sorts of souvenirs I still needed to pick up for friends and family. I was really looking forward to seeing Stream. He met me at the station as planned and we took the Metro to apartment 1070, 142 boulevard Massena, a high-rise in the thirteenth arrondissement that was being rented by Professor Édouard Roditi, poet, translator, art and literary critic, and short-story writer. Roditi and Stream had become friends at Bard College, and Roditi had invited Stream to stay with him for part of the summer. Stream had already been there for a few days before I arrived. I had never met Roditi but I had heard a lot about him, and, as a budding intellectual, I was daunted by the very idea of him. He was born in 1910 and had lived his life in avant-garde literary circles. He was part of the surrealist movement in the 1930s and had famous friends like Paul Bowles and Jean Cocteau. I was excited to meet him but, as it turned out, I never got that chance. He was not at home when we arrived at his apartment, and I caught a glimpse of him only once, in the early hours of August 2, 1990 — and at the time he was at a police station, behind bars in a holding cell.

Stream and I got to Roditi's apartment just before 6 p.m. Boulevard Massena is a wide and busy street in what used to be a largely working-class district of Paris, and when I went back to the apartment for the first time since the rape, in the summer of 2009, I was expecting to find a relatively upscale building at number 142, which is how I remembered it. But while the lobby has a feeling of grandeur, with a large mirrored wall and a giant glass chandelier, the interior of the building is sort of dingy, with cold, uncarpeted hallways and a bad paint job. Maybe that was the result of decades of neglect, or maybe it just looked plush to me twenty years earlier, compared to most of the hostels that I had been bunking in. The entranceway was just as I had remembered it, however, with a set of big glass doors at either end of the lobby. On the night of August 1, Stream and I made our way through them together before taking the elevator up to Roditi's apartment on the tenth floor. It was then that I met the man who would change my life forever, Robert Dinges, who Stream introduced as another houseguest. Robert (pronounced *row-bear*) spoke some broken English, and my French wasn't too bad, since I had taken French immersion in junior high. We all chatted a bit and Robert seemed pleasant enough. I learned later that he was Roditi's lover. I learned quite a bit about him later, mostly through assorted court documents. I know where he was born and I know his parents' names. I also know his date of birth—February 11, 1960, which means that when he raped me in the summer of 1990 he was thirty years old—exactly eight years older than me and fifty years younger than Roditi. I also learned that he had spent a handful of years in and out of jail, mostly for petty crime (a court document from 1990 reports that he had six convictions for theft and breach of trust). He was a big guy, tall and muscular, with dark hair and kind of bad skin but otherwise nondescript features. Stream and I chatted with him for a few minutes before he disappeared to the kitchen where he was preparing dinner for himself.

The layout of the small apartment is etched clearly in my mind. You walked in the front door and there was a galley kitchen directly ahead of you and a long hallway that extended to the right. The bathroom was at the end of the hallway and as you walked toward it there were two rooms that opened to the left, first the living room and then the bedroom. Stream and I decamped to the living room, where we would be sleeping on a pullout couch. We hung out for a few minutes and caught up while I started to unpack, but Stream was on his way out. He had a dinner date with Roditi and one of Roditi's friends. I remember being only half-invited to come along, but at the time I didn't mind because I was tired from traveling and preferred to just settle in and unwind. I could hardly wait to see Paris, but I had all week for that. Robert came into the living room and proposed that he make dinner for me as well, an offer that I happily accepted. Stream left shortly after that, around 6:45 p.m., and I took a shower to get cleaned up for dinner.

I remember feeling a bit vulnerable as I left the bathroom after my shower, conscious of the fact that there was a stranger in the apartment. I put my grungy shorts back on and wrapped a towel around my upper half before walking, unnoticed, back to the living room to change into fresh clothes for dinner. After I got dressed in a clean pair of shorts and a T-shirt I poked my head into the kitchen. Robert told me that dinner was almost ready and then offered me a cigarette. There was a small table in front of me, pushed up against the wall on the right side of the room, opposite from the stove where Robert was cooking, and I sat down at the chair that was closest to the doorway and smoked while he finished up. I think he made a salad and chicken of some kind, but the details of what we ate are now fuzzy. What I do remember, distinctly, is that he was drinking, moderately at first but after a while copiously. I think he had a glass of wine but he was also drinking a clear liquid, which I guessed was vodka. He offered me some and I declined, though he continued to press and so eventually I took a glass and nursed it. Our conversation during dinner was unremarkable. I talked a bit about my travels and, if I remember correctly, I asked him a few questions about where he was from. By the end of dinner his drinking was becoming excessive and it was starting to make me uncomfortable. He stood up to put a pot of coffee on the stove and then turned to me and, in his broken English, abruptly asked me a number of questions about

David. He asked, "Is David your boyfriend?," "Did you come here to be with David?," and then, pointedly, "Are you sleeping with David?" I deflected his questions with a growing sense of unease. I had gone from feeling uncomfortable to feeling almost unsafe, and I wondered if I should leave the apartment. It occurred to me then that I did not have a way of getting in touch with Stream to let him know where I had gone, but then I reasoned that I could just wait for him somewhere outside the building. Maybe there was a coffee shop on the corner and I could hang out there and keep an eye out for him. I would tell him about Robert's inappropriate questions and maybe even convince him that we should move into a cheap hotel, so as to avoid any further awkwardness.

I was sitting there trying to figure out some kind of a plan when Robert asked me directly if I would sleep with him. The niggling suspicion I had that something was off sharply intensified as he put this question to me, and I became genuinely scared. I didn't bother waiting for my coffee. I said "no," muttered a thank you for the dinner, and quickly left the kitchen. I hurried to the bathroom to wash my hands and think. For a moment I worried about how I was going to leave the apartment without appearing rude, but then I realized that it didn't matter how it looked—I had to get out of there. Not ten seconds later I left the bathroom and headed for the living room, where I had earlier left all of my stuff. I had to put on some shoes, and then I was going to grab some money and go, but I was too late. Robert was standing in the hallway, staring at me. As I walked toward him he ducked into the kitchen for a second and then reappeared and remained in the hallway, just in front of the doorway to the living room. Anxiously, I excused myself as I turned sideways to pass him, but he stopped me in my tracks.

What happened next took one hour and would turn out to be the single most transformative event of my lifetime. With my back to him as I turned to pass, Robert grabbed my hair with his left hand and wrapped his right arm around my upper body as he pressed a ten-inch-long kitchen knife forcefully into the left side of my neck. In case I didn't know what was going on he uttered in grammatically challenged English, "Do what I say, I kill you, shut up, I kill you." In a series of verbal exchanges that lasted no more than thirty seconds I tried to reason with him. My first thought was that if I told him that I would yield to his demands then he would put down the knife. In a feverish plea I consented, "OK, OK, I'll do what you want, just please put down the knife," but hearing my voice only made him angry. He pressed the knife harder into my neck while at the same time pulling my hair and repeating variations of what turned out to be his favorite phrase, "Shut up, I kill you." Again I started to respond but again he reacted with increased agitation. He was now practically ripping my hair out of my head. He moved the knife off of my neck and held it in front of my eyes, turning it from side to side, and said, "See this, I kill you, talk, I kill you, shut up, I kill you," and then he returned the blade to the left side of my neck.

It was at that point that it hit me like a truck that this man was not presently rational and that I was entirely at his mercy. I became acutely aware of the fact that he was not going to listen to anything that I had to say. This may sound peculiar, given that I was the focus of his brutal actions, but the feeling that came over me then was one of sheer invisibility. I realized that who I was, my personality, my character, my identity, were totally irrelevant to him and completely subsumed by his. It registered then that Robert was intending to rape me and kill me, and that there was nothing that I could do to stop him.

*

At that precise moment in the hallway when it dawned on me that I was going to be raped and killed I became stuck. Not literally, thankfully, as that would have put me in serious danger, but emotionally, and physiologically. I can close my eyes right now and remember that instant in Technicolor, as if it were yesterday. I can feel the knife's edge pressed hard into my neck and I can hear Robert's voice at the side of my head, commanding me. As I remember this I wince with the pain of losing my hair to his iron grip. This is a point in my life that is frozen in time, or at least was for many years, which should perhaps come as no surprise. This is precisely what research into psychological trauma tells us about what happens when our biological response to threat gets interrupted. Human beings have a fight-or-flight instinct, an automatic impulse to resist or escape danger. When we suspect that we are in serious trouble we naturally want to protect ourselves, to fight back, and if we can't do that, we want to run. When neither is possible the human nervous system becomes overwhelmed and chaotic, and we become paralyzed with our own powerlessness. Standing in the hallway, faced with Robert's mounting anger at my resistance, any impulse that I had to break free was squashed. A wave of helplessness rocked through me. I fell into a state of terror, and though my mind was racing the whole time I did not say another word during the events that followed.

*

Robert shoved me into the bedroom by my hair, which he was still gripping tightly. The bedroom was small and there wasn't a whole lot of room to move around. The bed was centered in the middle, the foot of it directly in front of us and the headboard to our right, pushed up against the back wall. There were a couple of feet on either side of the bed, and maybe three or four feet in front of it. We entered the room and immediately turned right, so that we were squeezed between one side of the bed and the closet, which was adjacent to the door. Robert let go of my hair then and told me to turn around to face him and take off my clothes. As I turned around he held the knife in front of my eyes and continued with his typical refrain, "Shut up, I kill you," which at this stage seemed unnecessary because I was no longer talking. I removed my clothes with numb fingers while he played around with the knife, impatiently. He then gestured for me to take off his pants. I bent forward and awkwardly fumbled with the buttons on his pants, which got him further riled up. I became even less visible, hunched over naked in front of him.

With his free left hand he forced me down onto the ground and replaced the knife on the left side of my neck and said, "Suck me." I was on my knees, eye level with his flaccid penis, as he began to push my head into his sweaty crotch with his free hand. I remember staring at his gnarled pubic hair, with his penis in my mouth, worried that I might throw up. I also remember thinking to myself that I should close my eyes and pretend that this was a guy I liked. Maybe I could escape what was happening to me by imagining that this was someone else's penis in my mouth. I even recall thinking of this cute guy that I had a crush on in high school. But these thoughts were fleeting; my eyes would not stay closed and I was not able to trick myself. Instead, it was his grotesque penis in my mouth, and it was becoming larger by the second. By my hair he pulled me again and again into him, and as he grew more excited he thrust his penis deeper down my throat, which made me gag, which made him equally agitated and aroused. His penis was now fully erect, and it felt enormous. I had no room for it in my mouth and although my choking seemed only to turn him on more, he eventually got tired of my efforts.

He took himself out of my mouth and jerked me up by my hair and pushed me onto the bed, so that I was lying sideways along the bottom of the bed. He told me to lie down on my back and without giving me a chance to catch my breath he climbed on top of me and began raping me vaginally. He draped himself over me and held himself up with his fists, the knife still in his right hand. I felt suffocated by the weight of his body, and in at least one respect the vaginal penetration was the most difficult to endure. It was rough and I suffered minor vaginal bruising from it, but it was less physically taxing than either what came before or what followed, and as a result it resembled real sex more than anything else that I had to put up with. And because my body was more compliant I felt that I was giving in somehow. But the vaginal raping did not last long, probably not more than a couple of minutes. It is possible that the relative physical ease of it wasn't stimulating enough for him. He pulled himself off of me and told me to turn over. I resisted for a second, gasped a wordless protest, and then turned over and lay on my stomach.

He mounted me from behind and without any hesitation (or lubrication) he rammed his fully erect penis into my anus. The pain was intolerable and I could not contain the shriek of agony that escaped from me then. His response to my cry was to lung forward and fold all his weight on top of me, and with his head level to mine he placed the knife in front of my eyes and stated as a matter of fact, "Scream, I kill you, cry, I kill you, shut up, I kill you." I bit my tongue and did what I could to stay quiet. He raped me anally until he ejaculated inside of me. By the time he was done I pretty much lacked all sensation in the rectal area, which by then was torn, bruised, and bleeding.

He got off of me and for a few seconds I held my breath, my mind racing, wondering if he was going to plunge the knife into my back. Instead he told me to turn over. I was still lying sideways at the foot of the bed and he was standing in front of the closet, near my feet, where I had taken off his pants, which he picked up off the ground with his free hand. I watched him as he got dressed and for a moment I entertained the possibility that he might just be done with me. But then he looked at me and began to utter his usual refrain and I realized that while he was indifferent to my earlier attempt to reason with him, he probably was not entirely irrational. He must have understood that I was now a serious threat to him, both as a victim and a witness to his crime, and consequently he would have had no intention of letting me walk away from this alive. Once again the awareness that I was about to die moved through me like a convulsion. But for a moment I was free from him and the sharpness of the knife at my neck and so I quickly scanned the room, not at all sure what I was looking for. What I saw was a telephone, perched on a night table that was just a few feet above my head, at the side of the bed opposite to the closet. Unfortunately, just as the phone caught my eye so did Robert, and I guess my faint hope registered with him because he reacted badly.

He walked around the room and dragged me by my hair up to the top of the bed, so that I was now sitting upright, facing the front of the room. He sat down next to me on the bed and with choked-back laughter in his voice he said something like, "You get away, I kill you." Then, like a bad Hollywood movie, he took the knife to the phone cord and sliced it in two. Still half-chuckling, he said, "You die." He then took the knife and traced the blade across my bare breasts, back and forth, up and down, about six times in total. I held my breath and suspended all thought, waiting for the knife to sink in. The absolute terror that I felt in those seconds still haunts me today. Of all the images in my head from that night, the one that I have had the most difficulty erasing is that of the knife traveling across my breasts, this way and that.

We were sitting so close to each other. Our faces were not more than two feet apart. I searched Robert's eyes in desperation for some connection, but came up empty. He carved faint scratches in my breasts but did not pierce the skin. Instead, he stood up and walked back around the bed to the door where my clothes lay and told me to get up and get dressed. I had a hard time walking but I did as I was told, my thoughts in a scramble over what was coming next.

Once I was dressed he directed me into the hallway and then into the living room, where all my stuff was. He waved the knife around and demanded that I hand over all my money, which was such a trivial request that I was taken aback by it. I walked over to my backpack and took out my money belt, which was something that all backpackers traveled with in the days before debit convenience cards and Interac. I had a small amount of cash in various currencies, as well as F300 and $700 in American Express traveler's checks. As I handed everything over to him I started to say something about how the checks would be no good to him without me around to sign them, but he cut me off and told me to shut up. In retrospect it seems strange that I tried to warn him about this, but I suppose I was worried that when he discovered that he couldn't use the checks without my signature he would be furious, and that I would bear the brunt of his anger.

My mind started to race again. Each minute that passed was a minute longer that I was not yet dead, and for as long as I was still breathing there was a chance that I could escape. As I was standing in front of him I furtively glanced around the living room looking for ideas, but couldn't see any easy way out. And then, as if to crush any kernel of hope, as if he could read my mind, Robert pushed me down onto my knees and told me to take off his pants. I was stunned with disbelief, and any notion I had that I might get out of the apartment alive evaporated. With the knife pressed hard into my neck I had no opportunity to hesitate. I did as I was told. The feeling of helplessness rippled through me again like a wave. He still had the knife in his right hand and with his left he grabbed my jaw and gripped it tightly, so as to keep me still while he jammed his flaccid penis into my mouth until it became hard. I was having trouble breathing and I began to gag, which again seemed to both stimulate and irritate him. He took his penis out of my mouth and told me to take off my shorts. There was a dusty rose armchair in the far corner of the living room. I had noticed it earlier when I was unpacking and although the color was faded I had commented to Stream that it was quite pretty. Robert demanded that I lean over the chair, face down, and he again raped me anally. It took him forever to ejaculate this time but I did not scream because by this point I was numb to any feeling.

When he finished he backed away from me and put on his pants and told me to get dressed. He also told me to put on my shoes and then he said, "You come with me, I kill you." It had not occurred to me until then that he was going to take me somewhere to kill me, rather than end it in the apartment, and the faint glimmer of hope that I had seen before returned. It seemed to me that the opportunities to escape would multiply if we left the apartment. But my hope was compromised by a moment of extreme panic. For as long as I was alive and in the apartment there was a chance that Stream or Roditi would find me. Maybe their dinner would be cut short and they would return unexpectedly soon. But if we left, how would anyone ever find me? How would they even know that anything bad had happened to me? There was a cut phone cord in the bedroom, but it could take a long while before someone even noticed that. If

I wasn't around, Stream might reasonably assume that I had decided to go out to take in some sights on my first night in Paris.

Stream and I had identical backpacking shoes, Birkenstock clogs, and I guess he had worn a different pair of shoes out for dinner because both of our clogs were lying on the floor of the living room. As I began to put on mine it struck me that I should slip on his instead, so as to leave him a clue that something was amiss. I thought I was being sneaky about it but I already had on one of my shoes, which I had to slip off in order to put on one of Stream's, and Robert caught me in the act. Surprisingly he didn't get too angry with me, he just made me put my shoes back on. He seemed distracted at this point, and anxious to get out of the apartment. He stepped out of the living room for a second and came back holding a short lightweight jacket. I'm not sure where he got it from but there must have been a closet or coat rack in the front entranceway. He put on the jacket while standing in the doorway of the living room and then he beckoned for me to join him there. He put his left arm around my neck and squeezed me into him while he placed his right hand, which was still holding the knife, under his jacket, around chest-high, and pressed it against me. He said, "We leave," and then "Speak, I kill you," and for emphasis he pushed the point of the knife into my side. He then opened the door and, just like that, we left the apartment.

Roditi's apartment was at one end of the building and the elevator was at the opposite end; in between there was a center block that contained lockers. A hallway formed a square around the block and apartments were dotted along the exterior. Robert held me close and we

walked together from the apartment, around the corner, and down the hall to the elevator. Being outside of
the apartment felt surreal. I was out in the world, yet
trapped inside my own private hell. As we walked past
each apartment I imagined the people inside them, right
there yet out of reach. I was still having trouble walking
and I was trying to stay focused on keeping step with
Robert. We reached the end of the hall and rounded a
corner and I could barely believe my eyes: there was a
woman standing there, waiting for the elevator to arrive.
My heart was pounding. Her back was to us and as we
walked toward her she briefly glanced our way and then
returned her stare to the elevator door. Robert now had
his arm so tightly around my neck that he was practically
strangling me. We stopped a few feet behind her and he
whispered in my ear "Speak, I kill you," and continued
to press the knife into my side. I didn't say a word but my
eyes were burning a hole in this woman's back, imploring
her to turn around, but she did not look at us again. Being
in close proximity to another person and not being able
to do anything about it was torture. The elevator arrived.
The woman got on first and then Robert and I walked on
as one and stood behind her, at the back.

  In a later interview with the police, this woman, who
also had an apartment on the tenth floor, reported that
our behavior seemed strange. She told them that we
had taken the long route to get to the elevator, as if to
avoid being noticed, and she also claimed to observe
that Robert had been holding me tightly and whispering in my ear. I suspect that, at least at a quick glance, we
looked a bit like a couple in love, him whispering sweet
nothings in my ear; this woman probably thought noth-

ing of our actions at the time. It's likely that only in retrospect would our behavior have seemed suspicious.

The elevator stopped once on the way down to pick
up someone before continuing to the lobby. The man
who got on was a dentist who practiced out of an apartment on the second floor of the building, which is where
I ended up not five minutes later, hysterical and waiting
for the police to arrive. I was surprised when I saw him
two years later at the trial. It hadn't crossed my mind that
he would be there, but had I given it any thought I would
have realized that, of course, he would have been called
on to testify. In his testimony then and in his original
statement to the police he also claimed that we looked
strange; he said that Robert appeared uncomfortable
and that I looked "feverish." I suspect that this interpretation of our behavior was also made in retrospect because we were together on the elevator for too short a
time for him to have fully grasped that something was
not right. Less than thirty seconds later we were all exit-
ing the elevator, making our way through the first set of
glass doors and then through the lobby toward the second set of glass doors that opened to the street.

There were a few other people in the lobby, and my
eyes bored holes through each one of them, but no one
paid any attention to us. The presence of other people
created a chance for escape that I knew I could not let
pass, but I had no idea how to take advantage of the moment, which was quickly evaporating. At the same time,
the presence of other people must have made Robert
nervous; we had followed the others through the first set
of glass doors but then he broke a stride and had us moving alone and fast toward the second set of glass doors.

Then the opportunity came. Robert's left arm was still wrapped around my neck as we walked up to the exterior doors, which swung outward to the street. Because his right hand was tied up with the knife he walked us toward the left hand door with the intent of using the upper part of his left arm to push it open. To accomplish this, however, he had to briefly loosen his hold on my neck, and in a split second that was wholly instinctual I ducked my head out from below his arm and took a step back. With the door half opened he stopped dead and turned to me, and for a couple of seconds we stood there in silence, our eyes locked on each other. I will never forget the angry look on his face. And then he turned and ran.

2: What Happened Next

The man who had entered the elevator on the second floor as it traveled down from apartment 1070, 142 boulevard Massena, on the night of August 1, 1990, paused in the lobby on his way out to talk with a woman who appeared to have been waiting there for him. They were standing behind me after I broke free from Robert. As soon as he took off, I screamed. I screamed and sobbed and cried out to this couple. I turned to them and grabbed them, literally, holding onto their arms, terrified they would disappear, and in between sobs I choked out that I had been raped by the man who had just run off. I said this in English first and then repeated parts of it, whatever I could, in French. I was hysterical but not incoherent, and they quickly understood the situation. They took me back inside the apartment block and up a flight of stairs to the man's apartment. We entered into a large room and they offered me a chair. The man, the dentist, picked up a phone and called the police while I sat there, crying hysterically, trying to catch my breath. In less than five minutes there were a half-dozen police officers at his front door. The officer in charge asked me a number of quick questions, in French (but, if I recall correctly, he also spoke a bit of English)—what happened, when, where, what did the guy look like, what did the knife look like, which way did he run—and then he sent out about half the group to go search for Robert. After that he sat down with me and, while the other officers were busy gathering information from the dentist and his companion, gently asked me more detailed questions. Between his English and my French he pieced together a picture of what had happened and, after making a couple of calls on his police radio, he asked me to accompany him and the remaining officers back upstairs. Without a moment's hesitation I refused. I was scared for my life, certain that Robert would be back at the apartment, waiting for me to return, waiting to kill me. This was, of course, illogical; if, by that point, Robert had managed to escape capture, he would be long gone, likely on his way out of town. The officer calmly explained this to me and, mortified by my irrationality, I decided to buy his story, which at some level I knew to be plausible despite my overwhelming suspicion to the contrary.

I thanked the dentist and his friend for their help and then we left his apartment and took the elevator back up to the tenth floor. This time surrounded by police, I walked the length of the floor along the hallway from the elevator back to Roditi's apartment. As we rounded the corner I had a shock: Stream was there, sitting on the floor, casually reclined against the apartment door with a book open on his knees. Apparently he had been late for his dinner date with Roditi and had failed to find him, so had returned to the apartment but without a key, sure that we would be there to let him in when he arrived. Evidently he had been sitting there for five or ten minutes, which means that we missed each other in the lobby by just minutes, perhaps even seconds (the thought of which still fills me with some dread over what Robert might have done with the knife that had been pressed into my side, had our timing been just a bit different). As we approached he looked up, startled, and the police, having no idea who he was, moved into action. I began sobbing again and tried to stop them from accosting him—*"ce n'est pas lui"*—he's not the one—I cried out. Stream was totally confused, but in a sentence I told him what had happened. And then my memory gets a bit fuzzy. I think at that point the police entered the apartment, but they would have had to break in, which strikes me now as unlikely. That said, I also half-remember going in with them to point out what had happened, and where, though I am not confident of this detail. I know for certain that I went back to the apartment the next morning. By then the rooms were taped off and there were assorted officials milling about, but I can't be sure that I also went back into the apartment that night. I do remember that I was not allowed to talk to Stream, who was being interrogated out of earshot by one of the police officers. I was not there for long, in any event. Stream was detained at the apartment by a couple of officers while I went along with the others in a police van to a local police station, where I was questioned again, this time in the office of a man who appeared to be the captain of the station, following which I was offered the chance, finally, to call home.

By now it was around 10:30 p.m. Paris time, which meant that it was 3:30 p.m. in Winnipeg. My first call was to my mom, at work, but she was in a meeting and unable to be reached. My dad was also at work and also in a meeting, but his secretary managed to track him down in a colleague's office and patched me through. My voice broke as I blurted out what had happened, and his broke in return. I don't imagine that I will ever forget how upset he sounded in that first call. I managed to get a grip of myself and I described to him, in rough outline, the events of the night. We quickly agreed that the best thing for me was to come home immediately. We spoke for about ten minutes, and once we hung up he went into action. My parents are nothing if not capable, and after getting ahold of my mom and breaking the news to her, they got on the phone with both the Canadian Embassy in Paris and Air Canada and began working behind the scenes to ensure my departure from Paris the next morning.

After I got off the phone with my dad I had to go to the hospital to get a rape kit done, which is basically a collection of evidence of a sex crime, including a blood analysis, miscellaneous swabs, and any relevant clothing. To this day I have no memory of actually being at the hospital and getting these tests done, although I do remember, however incongruously, walking around the police station wearing, under my shorts, mesh underwear that was adorned with a big maxi pad, which I had obviously gotten at the hospital in exchange for my underwear (which, having been stained with blood and semen, would have been kept as physical evidence of the crime). I also have in the rape file a number of medical documents dated August 1, 1990, which confirm my visit to the Hôtel-Dieu, the oldest hospital in Paris and one of the oldest in Europe, famously located on the Île de la Cité next to Notre Dame Cathedral. The hospital was founded by Saint Landry in 651 CE, and although its original architecture has been destroyed several times by fire, the present hospital, whose architecture dates from 1877, is a beautiful marble stone building. I went back there in the summer of 2009 and walked around the exterior of the building and roamed through the lobby, but nothing about the place felt familiar.

Although I still draw a blank about the hospital visit, my memory of the rest of the evening is pretty clear. At one point a couple of officers took me to a cafeteria in the station and bought me a coffee, which I drank while I smoked and listened to their conversation, and something to eat, which I left untouched. This must have been after I had returned from the hospital, because when we got back to the main office area Stream and Roditi were there, locked up in a holding cell just down the hall from the room where I had been interviewed.

This was the first time that I had ever seen Roditi, who looked old and wan, resting on a hard bench with his shoulders slumped down. As I approached the cell Stream jumped up to talk to me, but my attention was focused on Roditi. I was staring at him, angry and confused, tongue-tied but full of questions. Shouldn't he have known that Robert was a crazy violent rapist? And if so, why hadn't he warned Stream not to leave me alone with him? I was trying to catch his eye but he would not return my look. I am not sure what I wanted from him — recognition of some sort, an apology? In the end it didn't matter; he would not turn his gaze upward. To this day I wonder why. The sense that I had then, as I stood there in his plain view, unacknowledged, was that I had inconvenienced him. I experienced a piercing feeling of neglect, crystallized in that moment. To be fair, I have no idea why he would not look at me. Maybe he could not bear to face me because he was filled with remorse. Or maybe he felt no remorse at all. I will never know. He died one year later from injuries suffered in an accident in Spain, where he had been vacationing (according to his obituary in the *New York Times*), unjustly preempting my opportunity to see him at the trial and finally get the recognition from him that I had felt I deserved.

Stream and I talked for only a second, as the police hurried me along. I guess they didn't want us communicating, since, from what I could tell, both he and Roditi were being held under some suspicion at that stage. Apparently they spent the night together in the holding cell. I didn't see Stream again until the next morning, and then just briefly. He was being interviewed by an officer at a desk in a large, open room, which I passed through on my way out of the station, on my way home. I stopped to mutter a brief goodbye, but I could barely bring myself to look him in the eyes, my feelings toward him already a mess of hurt and anger over his role in the previous night's events. I think Roditi was also being interviewed at that time. I sort of remember seeing him seated at another desk, at the far side of the room, but that memory is not clear.

It had been a long night. After the trip to the hospital, and then the cafeteria, my parents called a few times, and so did a kind man from the Canadian Embassy. It was really hard to talk to my mom for the first time. I burst into tears as I told her what had happened and from thousands of miles away she tried to console me. I was aching for the comfort and security of my parents, and they reassured me that they were working to get me on a plane home the next day. By this point August 1 was over in Paris, and the police suggested that I try and get some sleep. As I had nowhere to go and no money, they offered me the station's "bedroom," a characterless room, empty except for a bed. I was initially relieved to have somewhere to lie down. I was beginning to feel the pain of the bruising on my backside. I was finding it hard to walk and I wasn't much more comfortable sitting upright. But when I realized that I would be left alone in this room I became scared for my life. I figured that Robert would be able to guess which police station I had been taken to, and I was convinced that he would come looking for me, find me, and kill me.

I relayed my fears in the form of a question to the officer who had escorted me to the room, who slowly shook her head in response. She patiently explained to me that this was the last place on earth that Robert would show his face. I knew that she was right and I was embarrassed by the irrationality of my reaction, just as I had been only hours earlier at the dentist's, when the police had asked me to accompany them back to Roditi's place. And yet, once again, I couldn't shake the feeling of terror that was coursing through me. In these instances I was experiencing my first few tastes of the disconnect that would deepen over the years between my cognitive and bodily responses to traumatic triggers. However well I might have understood that it would be insane for Robert to go anywhere near a police station, my body was plainly indifferent to this knowledge. The officer left me alone and I lay there until daybreak, with the lights on and my eyes wide open.

With the help of someone at the Canadian Embassy,

my parents convinced the Parisian authorities to let me go home the next morning. The police had wanted me to stay a couple of days longer, in case they caught Robert right away, but my parents insisted and prevailed. First thing the next morning a police officer took me back to boulevard Massena and walked me though the apartment, which was now buzzing with various officials doing things like dusting for fingerprints and taking pictures. I found the scene, which in retrospect looked like something out of a *Law & Order* episode, bizarre, and I observed it with a sense of detachment that had set in sometime during the night. I felt agitated but removed; I didn't feel sad or particularly upset. It was as if my emotional connection to the apartment and what had happened to me there had been turned off. I reclaimed my backpack and, if I remember correctly, I was given the chance to go to the bathroom to change out of the clothes that I'd had on all night.

And then I left Paris. We finished up at the apartment just before 9 a.m. and my flight was due to take off around 10:30 a.m., which was cutting it close, but I had a police escort to Charles de Gaulle Airport. Traffic was bad but the officer made up time by driving at a very high speed, mostly on the shoulder, with his lights flashing. When we got to the airport he came in with me, briefly, to check me in, again bypassing stalled lines, only to discover that my flight had been delayed a few hours. With time to spare I thanked him for his help, and then I was on my own. I made my way to my gate, where I found an empty chair to settle down in while I waited to board.

*

Those few hours of waiting at the airport felt like an eternity. I was exhausted, uncomfortable, and withdrawn. The tears that had flowed uncontrollably from me the night before, right after I escaped, and then when I saw Stream outside Roditi's apartment, and again later when I talked to each of my parents for the first time, had dried up. I felt dazed and overwhelmed. I had begun to disappear inside my head, but not in a quiet way. My thoughts were spiked with adrenaline. I could not relax. And I felt conspicuous, like I had a sign on my head that said RAPED in bold red letters. I felt so raw that it seemed inconceivable that someone could look at me and not know what had just happened to me. There I was in Paris's busiest airport, surrounded by people who seemed to be able to see right through me, feeling totally isolated.

After a couple of hours of sitting and waiting, fatigue got the better of me. The activity in my head slowed down and I closed my eyes. I even fell asleep for a few minutes, but some noise startled me awake and, without any warning, I experienced my first panic attack. My eyes opened to face a man who so closely resembled Robert, at least at first glance, that in a flash I was back in the apartment with the knife pressed against my neck and my life in the balance. My eyes clouded over and my heart began to pound and for a minute I was suspended in a traumatic memory. The complete surrender of my body to this memory felt like defeat, which is still how I feel each time I have a panic attack, although these days I understand better my body and its reactions to traumatic triggers.

Panic attacks can make us feel like our bodies are failing us. Abruptly, and seemingly for no good reason, your body is consumed by a cluster of symptoms that make you feel like you are in imminent danger. The heart palpitations, the shortness of breath, the hot flashes—all signs of a body's normal response to threat, tormenting you when you are out grocery shopping or at a dinner party or in a weekly staff meeting. Panic attacks can seem to come from nowhere because the intense fear is felt in the absence of any real danger, but over the years I have come to recognize a predictability and pattern in the panic. There are a number of specific cues that, when I am in a certain kind of environment, precipitate a traumatic memory, which makes my body react as if it were somewhere else.

Research into the causes of panic attacks has turned up no single definitive cause, but if we understand a panic attack as the body's response to the memory of a threatening experience, then we end up with a plausible biological explanation of the phenomenon. The body, behaving as if it is in danger, prompts a fight-or-flight response in the nervous system. The body readies itself for danger, in other words. A panic attack can thus be a sign of your body trying to protect you, but because you are presently not in any danger, panic attacks wind up being maladaptive. They often result in increased anxiety among those who suffer from them, which forms a kind of feedback loop, in turn increasing the frequency of the attacks.

Occasionally a panic attack will take me by surprise. In an unsuspecting moment my body will be flushed by a penetrating heat and I will stop breathing while my heart races away from me. When this happens I am reminded of my body's persistent unruliness, which bears the indelible marks of trauma, but for the most part I am attuned to the rhythm of the panic and its common triggers, which turn out to be fairly typical among those who suffer from severe anxiety. In a classic case, a panic attack will strike when I am feeling trapped. This feeling gets activated when I am in an enclosed public space, a small room, for instance, which for either social or professional reasons I feel unable to leave. Not surprisingly, those who suffer from panic attacks can develop agoraphobia, a fear of crowded spaces and enclosed public places.

Because panic attacks can be so debilitating, people who are prone to them often avoid triggering environments. They stay close to home and avoid social and work situations that might prompt an attack. I understand this impulse, but I am an academic philosopher and a university teacher by profession, which means that I face this kind of environment daily, which is not to say that I have panic attacks daily. Typically, though not always, I don't feel trapped when I am in a classroom teaching. I used to find this peculiar but I have come to understand that the feeling of being trapped has a lot to do with the control that I have (or at least believe that I have) over a particular situation or in a particular environment. I did have a lot of anxiety in the classroom when I first started teaching, because I was less self-assured and consequently felt less in control of a room full of students, but my confidence has grown over the years. What I have learned from this is that only when I am not in control or in charge—when I take the role of a bystander, for instance—am I likely to experience the array of emotions that trick my body into thinking that it is somewhere else.

Over the years I have developed a number ways of coping with these attacks. Because my body is being made to feel that it is elsewhere, my primary response to the panic is to try and ground myself in the present, using cognitive and bodily methods. For instance, I take the metaphor of grounding literally, and place my feet solidly on the floor to try and stay rooted to the here and now. I typically wear a watch, and I use this to have something to touch as a way of staying present, and to this end I also try and maintain eye contact with the other people in the room. This all helps to keep me grounded, and so does the quiet dialogue inside my head which is aimed at talking myself out of believing that I am in Paris in 1990. I tell myself where I am and how old I am, and I remind myself that I am currently safe. And, finally, failing all that, I rely on medication.

I have been taking clonazepam, which is a benzodiazepine often used to treat anxiety disorders, off and on for fifteen years. Benzos have sedative and muscle relaxant properties and they are mostly well tolerated, making them the drug of choice, at least traditionally, for treating anxiety disorders. They are also thought to have addictive properties, however, which helps to explain the rise in popularity over the last decade of selective serotonin reuptake inhibitors (SSRIs) as an alternate first-line treatment for anxiety disorders. There are many medications in the benzodiazepine family of drugs, with different pharmacological characteristics; clonazepam is a particularly long-acting one, and while it is not the most popular benzo (both lorazepam and alprazolam are more prescribed), it has worked well for me. There was a time when I was taking a daily dose, but these days I only take a pill as needed. Because I can often predict when I will be in an environment that will bring on an anxiety attack, I'll pop a clonazepam in anticipation. Sometimes I'll take one or two pills, which will actually slow down my beating heart, and other times I'll take a half a pill, which doesn't do much for my nervous system, per se, but has a pretty reliable placebo effect. And sometimes my heart will race notwithstanding, and I will have to push myself through the moment, taking air into my lungs and forcing myself to talk over a quivering voice.

*

In some cases, panic attacks can be traced to a genetic predisposition to acute anxiety. In my case, the panic seems connected to the way that my body holds and expresses trauma. I understand this, and I try not to judge myself when I succumb to an attack, but I still feel a bit defeated each time. And while the grounding methods and pills help to dampen the impact of an episode, the anticipation and experience of an out-of-place terror followed by a controlled managing of the terror can be exhausting. This was how I felt—exhausted and defeated—as I was recovering from my first panic attack in the early afternoon of August 2, 1990. Eventually my plane boarded and I left the City of Light, which, for me, for the last twenty years, has remained anything but.

There is no direct flight from Paris to Winnipeg, so I had to change planes in Toronto, where I came close to experiencing panic attack number two. I spent the flight from Paris reading Elie Wiesel's *Night*, his gripping account of the Nazi death camp horror, and I disappeared into his story and out of my own. I was just finishing the book when the plane touched down in Toronto, at which point my name was called out over the loudspeaker. I was asked to identify myself to a stewardess before de-planing. When I heard this my heart started to race and I became very confused. Why had they called my name? Who wanted to see me? I knew that it was impossible that Robert had taken an earlier plane to Canada and was waiting for me, in Toronto, in plain sight (and with the help of the airport authorities, no less), but, all the same, that was the first thought that flew through my mind. But if it wasn't him, then what was going on? Did the Canadian police want to talk to me? Was I in trouble of some sort? I didn't really have time to figure it out. Before I knew it a stewardess was escorting me through some gated area and into an office (or private room of some sort) where, to my surprise, I found my mom wait-ing for me. I had no idea that she was flying to Toronto to meet me but there she was, ready to take me home, and I folded with relief at seeing her. Finally, after a life-altering twenty-four hours, I felt safe.

*

I went to Paris twice in the two years following my rape. In September of 1990, Robert was caught in the South of France, in Nîmes, during an identity check, and di-rectly following that he was placed in custody in the notorious La Santé Prison in the fourteenth arrondisse-ment in Paris (ten years later, in 2000, the head doc-tor of the prison published a book about it, exposing its bad conditions, filth, illness, and high suicide rates). Un-believably, when Robert was caught he had in his posses-sion the knife that he had used on me. He was charged with rape under threat of weapon and theft, and he confessed to both crimes. At the beginning of December I received a letter from the Tribunal de Grande Instance de Paris, which requested that I travel to Paris to meet with a magistrate and give formal testimony about the night of the rape. The French government was offering to pay my way, and I convinced myself that I should go and try and make a vacation out of it, despite the fact that I had no desire to travel anywhere. I had been despondent since my return from Paris in August. Every day was a struggle. I was moving through life in a state of emotional disconnect. I woke up every morning with a sinking feeling as images of August 1 washed over me. I went through my daily routine in a kind of haze, unable to turn my thoughts away from the memory of the rape for any sustained period of time.

To make matters worse, in those first few months I experienced a near-constant stream of flashbacks, my body moving in tandem with the outline of each image. I began to develop a sequence of bodily tics. I would remember the feeling of my hair being wrenched out and my neck would scrunch up, as if to ease the pain; I would feel my jaw crushed by the grip of Robert's fist and I'd move my mouth around, as if to get the feeling back; I would feel my anus being ripped open and then squeeze my anus muscles shut, as if to prevent entry; I would feel the knife at the left side of my neck and fold my head down over the image of it, as if to protect my neck from further injury; and I would feel the knife scratching its way across my breasts and stop breathing, as if to steel myself for what was coming next.

Nights were particularly bad. I was restless, and I

would find myself staying up late, doing whatever I could do to avoid going to sleep. I was not quite scared of the dark, but once the lights were off there were no distractions to keep the flashbacks at bay. Over the last ten years I have learned how to manage my sleep better, how to coax myself into a state of calm, but back then I was simply surviving. I felt unstable, like I was riding on the tip of a wave, and it took all my focus to keep balance. The psychological trauma that would shape my emotional and physiological well being for the next decade was setting in.

Whatever challenges I was facing in my personal life, my academic life was going well enough. I was now in the second year of my undergraduate degree at the University of Manitoba, and school was turning out to be the one place where I was able to find some diversion from the rape and its aftermath. Initially, I had been drawn to philosophy because I was fascinated by questions about the nature of knowledge and reality, questions about what exists and about what we can know about what exists. I wanted to understand what made some beliefs worth holding and others not. I was also interested in making sense of ethical and value judgments; I wanted to know what made a good life good, and what sorts of things in life we should value and why. Philosophy is the study of these kinds of fundamental problems, and analytic philosophy, which is the sort I practice and which is dominant in North America, England, and various other pockets of the world, is distinguished from other disciplines that are concerned with similar questions by its reliance on logic and rational argument to advance its claims. The method of analytic philosophy has produced some of the greatest ideas of all time, but it is not a discipline that requires much self-awareness, at least, not typically. It does not ask philosophers to be attuned to their emotional responses to its subject matter or to have a personal or experiential connection with it (which is decidedly not to say that certain areas of philosophy aren't enhanced by such a connection). In other words, it is possible to be a world-class philosopher without looking inward, and so, incidentally, I found myself in a discipline that suited me perfectly. Although my commitment was at times perfunctory I had been genuinely seduced by the rigor and rationality of philosophy's analytic method, and I was relieved to be able to retreat into the safety of a world of logic and reason, a domain wholly external to mine.

When I was studying philosophy I could disappear into the realm of abstract ideas and pretend that there was nothing wrong with me, but I was unable to keep up this pretense outside of school. I was struggling in most aspects of my personal life. As the weeks and months wore on it became clear that there would be no "bouncing back" for me, and I became ashamed about my inability to recover quickly. When December rolled around and I received the request from Paris asking me to come and meet with a magistrate, the rape was four months behind me and I felt strongly that I should be over it already. I had made a conscious decision to just get on with things, so to speak. I decided that the fact that I had been raped would not stop me from doing anything I might have otherwise done, which is how I managed to convince myself that I should go to Paris and make a vacation out of it. I would never before have passed on a free trip anywhere, let alone to Paris, and so I talked myself into wanting to see all the sights that I had not had the chance to visit when my trip had been cut short the previous summer. I was clawing my way around the pain of the rape, shoving it aside, pretending that it didn't exist. This was a valiant effort and I persisted in it for close to ten years, but it was misguided. No matter how hard I pushed forward I could not leave the trauma of the experience behind me.

*

I flew to Paris alone, but at least I had the sense to arrange to meet friends there. My new Dutch friend met me for the duration, and a longtime family friend who lived in the South of France came for a few days as well. My most vivid memory of that trip is of the day I arrived. We had made reservations at Hôtel Saint André des Arts, a decent three-star hotel in the sixth arrondissement—one room, three beds. I was the first to arrive. It was early morning when I checked in, and our room wasn't yet ready. The hotel is located in the center of a busy tourist area just off rue Saint-Germain-des-Prés, with coffee shops and restaurants on every corner. Since I had some time to kill I decided to go to the nearby Café Le Conti on rue de Buci and have an espresso while I waited for the room and my friends. It was January 1, 1991, and I took a seat on the outdoor patio, even though it was around 0°C. It had been something like −30°C. in Winnipeg the day before, so it felt balmy to me. The charming cobblestone streets were full of people stumbling home from New Year's Eve parties that had run late, and I remember sitting there alone, watching the crowd, bursting with anxiety. The feeling was crushing, for while at some level I understood that I was not in any imminent danger, sitting outside Café Le Conti in the early daylight hours on a busy corner of one of the enchanting streets of Paris, I felt scared for my life.

This was becoming a familiar, however peculiar, experience, for it was obvious to me even at the time that I was not in any jeopardy, sitting there, drinking my espresso, watching the beautiful people of Paris pass me by. I could appreciate the fact that I was perfectly safe, and yet it was as if my body had a mind of its own. It did not seem to matter what I believed, I simply did not feel safe. I could not have articulated it then, but my body was responding as if it were under threat, even though it patently was not. It was as if the part of my brain that controlled my body did not know that I had escaped from Robert and that I was no longer in serious peril. All it seemed to know was that I was back in Paris. And so, just like the night I had spent in a Paris police station the summer before, I was experiencing a marked disconnect between what I consciously understood to be true and a different truth that my body unconsciously held. This is one of the most persuasive facts that I have come to learn about psychological trauma, which is that our autonomic bodily responses to trauma fail to neatly track our consciously held beliefs about the world.

Throughout that entire trip I experienced a heightened state of anxiety that I could never quite come down from. In the language of posttraumatic stress disorder (PTSD), this is called hyperarousal, and it is characterized by a nervous system that is on high alert. I was vigilant, always aware of my surroundings, and constantly on guard. I was unable to let my defenses down. I continued to have trouble sleeping, but now I was also jumpy and easily startled. And worst of all, I was having trouble breathing. I have been plagued with this affliction ever since I was raped. In moments of high anxiety I cannot catch a deep breath. My breathing remains attenuated, riding on the surface. This is wretched. It pulls me into myself and forces me to monitor every breath I take, thereby constraining whatever else I might be doing. It requires a degree of self-preoccupation that is inhibiting. The problem has gotten better over the years, and nowadays, weeks, even months pass without me ever noticing a shallow breath. But to this day it remains one of my clearest indications that my body is in distress.

Sometime in the middle of this trip I met with a magistrate named Sabine Foulon, and I had a Parisian lawyer escort me to her office. Back in September, my dad had made contact with a couple of bilingual lawyers at a firm in Paris. My parents were devastated by what had happened to me and desperately wanted someone to take responsibility for it. My dad wrote to these lawyers to inquire whether there was any way that I could file for damages or claim compensation from the French government. We were told (wrongly, as it turned out) that as a Canadian citizen, I was ineligible for any kind of compensation. A couple of months later, when we learned that Robert had been caught and that I was to travel to Paris to testify, we again contacted one of these lawyers, this time to check whether I now needed legal representation. He told us that while I didn't need a lawyer I would benefit from having one, and so for a time we retained his services. Again, this was bad advice, but on that day in January 1991, I was happy to have someone meet me at the magistrate's office and keep me company while I testified as to what had happened the previous summer.

I went to Paris again in May 1992 for Robert's sentencing trial, and this time my dad came with me. I don't remember having a lot of anxiety during that trip, despite the fact that I was about to face my rapist in court. Having my dad with me calmed my nerves. Over the years it has become clear to me that while being in an unfamiliar environment can be challenging, being alone in an unfamiliar place can trigger me into a state of hyperarousal. But this was not something that I was consciously aware of in those first few years following the rape, and as a result I made a number of bad decisions during that time.

*

Sometime in the afternoon of August 2, 1990, shortly after I left Paris, Stream was released from police custody. He stayed in Paris for a bit and then roamed around Europe, hitchhiking aimlessly in a state of what he later described to me as utter despair until mid-August, when he was booked to fly home. He did not call me once in that entire time. I did not hear from him until he was back in upstate New York, sixteen days later. That was an intolerably long period of waiting to hear the phone ring, and I could not make sense of why he had not called. I was embarrassed by this apparent lack of concern, and didn't quite know how to handle the intense feelings that it stirred up in me. I remember making up excuses on his behalf to my parents, who were even less understanding. Maybe he was still being held in police custody, I suggested, but as each day passed that story became less and less plausible, and I became increasingly hurt and angry. I had been desperate to hear his voice and feel his support, but I had also wanted to talk to him because I was seething; I had a lot of questions, and I wanted some answers. Who the hell was Robert? How well did Roditi know him? What did Roditi have to say about him? Was Roditi sorry for what had happened? How long had they been lovers? What sort of information did Roditi give the police about him? How much time had Stream spent with Robert before I had arrived? Were they buddies? Had the three of them had dinner together? Gone out on the town? Shared some laughs?

When Stream finally called I was almost too angry to speak to him. He told me that he had spent the previous two weeks overcome with remorse. He apologized for not calling earlier. He explained that I had looked so angry when I had said goodbye to him at the police station that he had assumed I would not want to hear from him, at least not right away. He had also run out of money and couldn't afford to make the call, and the circumstances were such that he didn't think he should call collect. He simply had no idea that I had been sitting at home, waiting for a call day in and day out. His reasons for not calling didn't cut it as far as I was concerned, but in the end it didn't matter. None of his answers to my questions were of any help, because what I really wanted was for him to undo what had been done. I also desperately wanted some explanation as to why Stream, who had been living in the same apartment as the man who had savagely raped and almost killed me, had not been able to see that Robert was a dangerous and violent criminal. It was totally unreasonable, but I wanted to know why Stream had been unable to predict what would happen if he left me there alone, and why he had done nothing to prevent it. It was not fair and I knew it, but it was hard for me not to blame him.

*

Within one month of being raped, I began dating a guy in Winnipeg. He and I had had a couple of romantic encounters the spring before I left for Europe, and basically we picked up where we left off when I got back. It was an experiment for me, part of my plan to not let the rape butt into my life, and it was an unequivocal failure. I had sex with this guy on a regular basis for nine months and every single time I reexperienced the violence of the rape. My body was in a perpetual state of flashback. He would caress my breasts, and I would imagine the knife carving out scratches on them; he would touch my hair, and I would cringe at the memory of it being pulled out. His penis would rub up against my backside, and my body would freeze up. Oral sex was particularly triggering. I would go down on him and he would touch my head, a loving and intimate gesture, and I would gag from the violence of the memory that brought up. The intensity of the flashbacks was heightened by the fact that, just like during the rape, I was mute throughout the experience. I was simply incapable of putting words to what I was going through, and although this time the silence was of my own doing, I didn't see that I had any other choice. I did not tell him that I had been raped. I was not ready to talk about it, and the only other alternative was to stop having sex, which, understandably, is what a lot of women do, but I had stubbornly refused to admit that the rape had compromised my sexuality. Instead, I became expert at masking my discomfort, and as a result my boyfriend didn't suspect a thing. I tried to enjoy myself, and I was successful at least some of the time (oddly, the flashbacks were present even if I was physically aroused). But for the most part, sex was a disaster. My relationship with my body was quickly becoming one of estrangement.

The only person who I felt comfortable talking to about what I was going through was Stream. Although I directed a lot of my anger toward him in the first few months following the rape I got tired of always being angry, and it got in the way of my being able to turn to him for support. I wanted the emotional dissonance that had hijacked my inner life to disappear, and so I buried my anger and reconciled with him. But our relationship was strained, scarred by what had happened to me and by his role in it. We decided that we needed to see each other again. Stream and I now had an unbreakable connection, yet a chasm had opened between us, and it took years before it became clear that it was too deep to traverse. Back then we thought we could work through it. We agreed that I would visit him at his parents' place in the spring, once school ended for the year. This would be my second trip since the rape, having already returned to Paris in January. And just as I had convinced myself then that my adventurous spirit had not been killed on the night of August 1, I again adopted the same false bravado. And so, ten months after that fateful night in Édouard Roditi's apartment on boulevard Massena, I decided to drive, alone, halfway across the country to New York to visit Stream.

*

One of the typical symptoms of PTSD is avoidance. It is not uncommon for someone who has lived through a traumatic experience to steer clear of anything (or anyone) that reminds her of the event. But the impact of extreme trauma and acute stress has contradictory effects on our behavior around traumatic triggers. Whereas a survivor might go out of her way to avoid something that reminds her of her trauma, she may also attempt to relive the event through familiar triggers. One way to understand this sort of reenactment (what Sigmund Freud at one time called the "repetition compulsion") is to see it as an attempt by the survivor to master her feelings surrounding the event. She relives it with the hope—unconscious or not—of changing the outcome this time around.

If this is right, then it may help explain why rape survivors sometimes put themselves in high-risk situations (which, in turn, may help to explain the statistic that women who had been victimized before are more likely to be raped again—seven times more likely than those who haven't, according to one study). If a survivor can replay certain aspects of the traumatic event with the hope (however unconscious) of changing the outcome, then there is a chance that the emotional power of a trigger can be deflated.

I fell into a pattern of reenactment over and over again in the years following the rape. Not speaking during sex was one obvious example of this. Putting myself in an unpredictable situation by driving alone across the country was another. At the time I was able to convince myself (and my parents, who weren't keen on the idea) that it was perfectly safe. And I did take certain precautions. I didn't drive late at night, for instance, and I stayed in decent-looking roadside motels. But the whole experience was layered with anxiety. Every time I stopped for gas or lunch or checked into a motel, I felt at risk. I was constantly looking over my shoulder. I could not catch a deep breath. And although I tried to convince myself that I was having fun by listening to good music and taking pictures of the awe-inspiring Canadian Shield, it was an exhausting drive.

Sometime near the end of this trip I had a peculiar phone call with my parents. I had been calling home regularly to touch base, first from phone booths and motel rooms, and then later from Stream's parents' place. I have a vivid memory of one of these calls, during which my mom was gushing with concern and affection. It felt out of place. We had already talked numerous times since I'd left Winnipeg and none of our previous calls had this tone to them. I could not make sense of it and as soon as I pointed it out my mom became restrained, but for the remainder of my trip the character of our calls continued to be flavored by this kind of demonstrativeness on my parents' part. Eventually I decided that they were just missing me, my absence a painful reminder of how close I came to losing my life in Paris ten months earlier.

This was nearer to the truth than I had imagined. On the night that I got home from my trip my parents called me into the den for a private conversation. They both looked very serious. They told me that while I had been out of town my dad had received a call from our lawyer in Paris who had informed him that Robert had undergone medical tests in prison, and that it had been discovered that he was HIV-positive. I remember hearing my parents talking but not really taking in what they were saying. It seemed unreal. The words floated in front of me but they had no purchase. My parents, on the other hand, were visibly upset. This news was dire. It was 1991, when HIV/AIDS was considered a death sentence—an untreatable, terminal disease. As a matter of procedure, I had been tested for HIV three months after the rape, and the test had come back negative. Most people who are infected with HIV turn infectious quickly, although it can take six to twelve weeks for HIV antibodies to develop in a person's blood, which is why it is recommended that people wait three months after a possible exposure to get tested. However, in very rare cases these antibodies can take up to six months to become detectable, and in even rarer cases it can take longer than that, and so I had to get another test, which my parents had gone ahead and scheduled for the next day.

*

In the ten days between being tested and getting the results I grew certain that I was HIV-positive. Partly that was due to the fact that Robert's semen had mixed with my blood around the anal tearing, which put me at high risk for transmission, and partly it was due to my conviction, which had been hanging like a noose around my neck since the summer before, that I was deeply, and irrevocably, unlucky.

And then there was another problem. After getting the all clear following the first HIV test I had been using the pill as a form of birth control. By the time that I learned that Robert was HIV-positive I had been sleeping with my boyfriend for months without a condom. And this meant that, however unwittingly, I had put his life in danger. Even though I dreaded the idea of telling him about the rape, I now felt an overriding moral obligation to do so.

At some point while I was waiting for my test results, I left the cocoon of my basement bedroom in my parents' house to sit down with him and tell him my story. As I started to talk I was overcome with panic. My heart began to pound and the room started to close in around me, but the waves of anxiety eventually subsided and I managed to get the story out. Despite the fact that I had potentially put his life at risk he responded to me in the most compassionate way and with heartfelt kindness. Even though I was still wracked with guilt, I felt supported and cared for, and telling him had an unanticipated but happy consequence: it altered the complexion of our sex life. Knowing the details about the rape allowed him to be mindful of the sort of touching that triggered me. We stopped seeing each other not too long after that, but I learned something important from the experience, which was that if my romantic partner knew that I had been raped, it could mitigate my flashbacks during sex.

Aside from that one outing, I spent those ten days in a trance-like state in my bedroom. I was overwhelmed and couldn't pretend otherwise, so I just hid out. I simply could not talk myself out of believing that I had become infected with HIV, even though the odds of me getting a positive test result beyond three months after contact were exceptionally low. But the fact that there was any chance drained me of all hope. The idea that Robert would have managed to kill me in the end seemed like the only plausible denouement to the story.

Although I did not know this at the time, the feeling that I had then and was unable to shake—the expectation of catastrophe—is typical among people who have survived traumatic events. Having experienced an unexpected terror, trauma survivors fear for the worst, their nervous systems caught in a constant state of expecting harm. I found it hard to even entertain the possibility that I was HIV-negative. I wrote out a will—who would get my books, my clothes, and whatever other meager possessions I had accumulated by the age of twenty-two, and I bided my time. Then, on June 12, 1991, a beautiful spring day, my dad and I returned to the doctor's office. I waited outside, chain-smoking for an excruciatingly long half-hour before my name was called and I got the news that I was HIV-negative. I saw the relief that surged through me mirrored in my dad's expression, and in that moment, I felt free.

*

Exactly eleven months later, on May 12, 1992, close to two years after he changed my life forever, I faced Robert Dinges in a courtroom in the Palais de Justice, located across the road from the Hôtel-Dieu on the Île de la Cité. I had returned to Paris to give a victim impact statement at Robert's sentencing trial, again at the expense of the Parisian government and this time accompanied by my dad. We arrived a few days early and planned to stay for a total of one week (once more, forcing myself to take advantage of a free trip). Although I had some anxiety about seeing Robert again, I wasn't a total wreck. As I said before, having my dad with me helped to steady my nerves.

My memory of that day in court is fairly clear. The Palais de Justice, like all Parisian landmarks, is a beautiful and historic building, and the room that we found ourselves in was capacious, wrapped in dark wood and characteristic European charm. I sat on one side of the room with my dad, a translator, the *procureur général* Jean-Claude Thin, and assorted court clerks. At the front of the room was an expansive platform, and sitting behind it were three robed jurists, two men and one woman. And sitting directly across from me were Robert and his lawyer. It was disquieting to see him again. I don't think he looked over at me even once during the proceedings—at least I don't remember catching his eye—but I stared at him throughout, sort of victoriously (an "aha—you're going to jail for what you did to me" look), though I was not feeling very victorious. I had not been quite sure what I would feel, going in that day. People say that facing one's assailant in court provides an opportunity for closure, but I guess that depends on what "closure" means. If it means something like emotional peace, then I wasn't feeling any closure. Still, the act of making public a private trauma in a court of law can be powerful, and there was certainly some satisfaction in watching the man who had wronged me being held accountable for that wrong.

Robert had pleaded guilty to the charges, so the trial was strictly a sentencing trial. It lasted for half a day, and I had been summoned, not to testify about what happened to me on the night of August 1 (the court had those details, which were in my deposition in the pretrial *indictment*), but rather to talk about the impact that the crime had had on me. I was there as a *partie civile*, which, in rough translation, is a civil plaintiff at a criminal trial. I stood at the center of the room and spoke into a microphone, giving my testimony in English and broken French, stopping after each sentence to let the translator correct whatever misunderstandings I had managed to convey. I talked about the physical injuries I had sustained during the rape, which had faded within a few weeks, save for the scar tissue that formed as a result of the anal tearing (and which to this day remains prone to bleeding, an interminable reminder of the rape), and I talked about my broken nerves, which, two years later, weren't getting much better. I had not yet started on anything resembling a road to recovery, and so I did not have handy the language of PTSD, but I still managed to describe myself as having been psychologically traumatized. I talked about my relentless anxiety, the trouble that I'd been having sleeping, and the bombshell that hit when I learned that Robert was HIV-positive. I told the jurors how my sex life had been corrupted and how relationships in general were difficult to sustain. And I talked about my inability to feel safe in even the most benign situations, like walking down a busy street during midday, and I described the frustration of these recalcitrant emotions—of feeling afraid despite knowing that I was in no danger.

The *procureur général*, Monsieur Thin, had instructed me to be as detailed as I could be to the jury about how the rape had impacted me, and so I told them about this one case, in particular, which epitomized my wayward emotions and their immunity to reason. I used to drive a Honda Accord hatchback. I loved that car, but in the years following my rape, whenever I drove alone—particularly at night but even in the middle of a bright, sunny day—I became sick with fear that there was someone hiding in the hatchback, waiting to attack me. My heart would race and I would check the rearview mirror incessantly for potential movement in the back of the car. I would even get out of the car, periodically, and circle around it, just to make sure that there was no one crouched down, hiding in the hatch. But this gave me only a momentary respite from my fear, which would return as soon as I got back to the driver's seat. I knew that my fear was groundless, but just like the night I spent at the police station in Paris and the morning at Café Le Conti six months after that, I could not reason myself out of the expectation that there was someone waiting to attack me. I remember feeling mortified as I told this story in court. I happened to lock eyes with one of the jurors while I was talking. His expression was filled with pity as I described my life in scenes that were "before" and "after," and although I am sure that he meant to be sympathetic, his pity made me feel pathetic.

My dad had come with me to Paris for moral support, but during a break in the trial a court clerk approached us to ask him if he would also be willing to testify as to my well-being, and so he, too, with the help of the translator, stood before the jurors and repeated much of what I had already said, but from a parent's perspective. The dentist had also been summoned to testify. It felt good to see him again, and it gave me (and my dad) a chance to thank him for his help two summers earlier. At one point during the proceedings the female judge, who appeared to be the main juror, called out Roditi's name, as a question. I was surprised; I had not been expecting to see him and I began to turn in my chair toward the entrance of the room, searching, but as I did one of the court clerks declared, "*Il est mort.*" Roditi was dead. I was shocked. I had no idea he had died, and I took it personally. It was like a slap in the face, like he died just so that he wouldn't have to answer for his role in what had happened to me. It felt like he got the last word. (If memory serves, Stream had also been asked to testify, but they hadn't offered to pay his way and he couldn't afford to make the trip.)

Robert did not address the court directly. Instead, his lawyer spoke on his behalf. Robert had confessed to his crimes when he was first picked up in Nîmes in September 1990, though he denied then that he had intended to kill me. Now, close to two years later, his lawyer still maintained that Robert was not a killer, and he also claimed that Robert had no memory of what he had done to me because he was seriously intoxicated at the time. The lawyer then went on to chart Robert's difficult childhood and his abusive father, and his subsequent dependence on alcohol and drugs. In a few short hours, following a couple of long years, the trial was over and—just like that—the court announced that Robert was to be sentenced to eight years in jail. *Huit ans.* Eight years. Robert was removed from the courtroom and just like that, it was over.

*

As this news sank in one of the court clerks approached my dad and me to offer directions to the claims office, where we were to go to file for a reimbursement for my travel expenses. The translator was still milling about, and through him the clerk told us that since my dad had testified, he too would be eligible to claim his travel expenses, which felt like further vindication. Finally, it seemed, things were going my way. At this point Monsieur Thin joined the discussion. We had had some contact with him before the trial; in particular, he wrote to inquire about the results of my second HIV test. He had been kind and compassionate to me that day in court, and when he approached us afterward he told us (again through the translator) that as a *partie civile* I was eligible to file for compensation for damages. My dad and I were surprised to learn this, since a year and a half earlier our Parisian lawyer had told us just the opposite. I still have the letter, written on his firm's letterhead, which states that, as a Canadian citizen, I was ineligible to file for damages of any sort. The lawyer had poorly advised us instead to sue Robert (a penniless criminal), which we did not do.

We got more bad advice when we contacted the lawyer after learning of Robert's capture in the fall of 1990, which was that we should retain his services. He had said that while it was not crucial that I had a lawyer working on my behalf, it would help to ensure Robert's conviction on the charges that he was facing (at the time, we hadn't known that Robert would enter a guilty plea). Once again, the opposite was true. In the first place, this was the government's case to try, not mine. Moreover, from what we found out later, having legal representation at the trial could have compromised my status as a *partie civile*, which would have meant, first, that I couldn't claim damages, but more importantly, it might have made me ineligible to testify at the trial. That would have been disastrous, since we had been told in advance of the trial that my victim impact statement was absolutely essential to the sentencing process. Thankfully, by the time the trial date came around we had already ended our relationship with the lawyer.

*

One month after the trial I received a letter from Monsieur Thin with details on how to file for an indemnity. When we had spoken directly following the trial he had told me that when I submitted my claim I would have to pick a dollar value for damages suffered. How was I supposed to come up with this number? I had wondered aloud. The trauma of the rape was so severe that it was hard to believe that it had been almost two years since that fateful night, and harder still to know how to put a dollar value on my damage, which had been awkwardly conspicuous at the sentencing trial.

Monsieur Thin's response was delicate but firm: I should choose a number that wasn't so high that it scared off the adjudication committee, but not so low that it undervalued the harm done to me. He suggested that an appropriate figure would be F50,000 (about CA$10,000). In his letter he included a *note d'information* on *cas d'indemnisation par la fonds de garantie des victimes d'infractions pénales*. He had highlighted all the relevant bits, which my dad's bilingual colleague translated for us. We followed the instructions and submitted a claim.

Months went by before we heard anything back, but then, in December 1992, I received a letter from la Commission d'Indemnisation des Victimes d'Infractions de

Paris advising me that the commission had scheduled a hearing to decide my claim on March 5, 1993. I was asked to attend the hearing and give a statement, but this time I would have had to pay my own way, so I declined the invitation. Instead, I sent along a sworn affidavit (in French) testifying to the damage claim I had submitted. Over that winter and spring I received two more letters about the hearing, which had been rescheduled twice and eventually took place on June 18, 1993.

Later that summer I received a letter from the Fonds de Garantie, informing me that a decision had been rendered to award me the funds. I have the minutes of this decision (taken by the secrétariat-greffe of the Tribunal de Grande Instance de Paris), which recount the verdict in my favor of the commission at the hearing, as well as the verdict of the Fonds de Garantie and le ministère public, who had concurred. I had been awarded the full amount, F50,000. It wasn't a lot of money—it wasn't going to change my life—but it was something. By then it had been three years since the rape, and despite all my attempts to bury the experience not a day went by that I didn't endure its repercussions. But maybe, I thought, maybe this was the closure that I had needed. Finally, there would be no more letters from Paris, no more nagging reminders of that drawn-out hour in Roditi's apartment. Perhaps now I could close the book on Robert Dinges.

*

I had graduated with an undergraduate honors degree in philosophy earlier that spring. As part of my campaign to ignore the aftermath of the rape I moved out of the safety of my parents' house and was living on my own.

I was also about one year into a five-year relationship with another philosophy student, a wonderful guy who I was never able to trust. Our relationship did not have a clean beginning. There had been some overlap with exes; in particular, he cheated on me with a recent ex-girlfriend of his, and this left me plagued with suspicion and a sense of impending betrayal from the very start of our relationship. This fed directly into my catastrophic thinking and it played out in the daily course of our lives, and it was intolerable for us both. He would be out of my sight for ten minutes—to go the local grocery store, for instance, to buy some milk—and I would be convinced that he was using the pay phone in the store to call his ex-girlfriend. We could be at a rest stop on some high-way halfway across the country or at our local pub, it didn't seem to matter. If there was a period of time dur-ing which I could not account for his exact whereabouts, I felt at risk. And whatever reassurances he offered gave me only a passing relief from my suspicions; my vulnera-bility could not be appeased.

Despite this scourge of insecurity, our first few years together were teeming with love and romance. We spent all of our time together and then some. We had many late nights and lost weekends, drinking, playing cards with friends, watching hockey, and drinking some more. He had also completed an undergraduate degree in philoso-phy from the University of Manitoba and was getting set to do an MA in philosophy there in the fall. I wasn't sure what I was going to do. I was living off student loans. I had not applied to grad school, I didn't have a job, and my inner life was wearying. I felt harassed by the relent-less insecurity that tormented me throughout our relationship and also by the intrusive thoughts and sleepless nights that had carved deep lines in my posttraumatic existence. And then, in the middle of the summer, I got this windfall of cash, which appeared to be a solution to at least some of my problems. I didn't need to work. I could spend the year traveling instead. I could go back to Europe and try again. This seemed like a fitting use of the F50,000, and I convinced myself that it was the right thing to do. The plan was to go overseas alone in the fall and eventually, when he finished school, my boyfriend would come meet me and we would spend the summer traveling together. I gave a couple of months' notice on my apartment and got set to leave in October. But I never left. I could not bring myself to get on a plane and go back to Europe. And I could not admit the truth — to myself or to anyone else — which was that the idea of going overseas and traveling alone filled me with dread. I used one excuse after another to delay my departure, and before long I had moved in with my boyfriend, gotten a job, and settled back into life in Winnipeg. I put in an application to do an MA in philosophy at the University of Manitoba for the following fall, and I bided my time. But by the spring of 1994 I had run out of excuses to delay my trip and I finally booked a ticket. I decided to start my trip in the South of France, in Aix-en-Provence, where an old family friend was living. He was the brother of the woman who had met me in Paris two years earlier. She was planning to come for a short visit, as well, following which I would go to London for the first time. My plan was to find casual work there for a couple of months while I waited for my boyfriend to show up.

I flew to Marseille with a connection in Paris, and

as soon as the plane touched down on French soil, my breathing became shortened. I was doubled over with anxiety, which I tried to mask by looking cool. I had dark circles under my eyes due to a combination of my natural skin tone and perpetual lack of sleep, which I accessorized with a beat-up purple leather jacket and a cigarette dangling from my mouth. From Marseille I took a bus to Aix-en-Provence, where I stayed with my friend for just under a week, housebound, as it turned out, tethered to his toilet, racked by a fever with nausea and diarrhea. At the time I wrote this off to a bad falafel, but it seems obvious to me now that this stomach flu was my body's way of expressing its trauma. Not all stomachaches have a psychological cause, of course, but it would have been very triggering for me to be back in France. Just the clatter of a French accent made my heart skip. And although to the best of my knowledge Robert was in jail, he had look-alikes everywhere. My sick stomach enabled me to stay inside, where it felt safe.

I had spent the previous year telling myself that enough was enough, that the rape and its aftermath were truly and forever behind me, and I had finally started to believe it. I had no idea that the anxiety consuming my body was connected to the fact that I was back in France. Had I been aware of this I might have been able to consciously process the experience; but since I wasn't, my body took over. My stomach eventually calmed down, and a week later I left for London.

*

Being alone in London was easier than bunking with a friend in France, but not by much. I wonder now how I was able to convince myself then that I was having fun. Traveling alone in Europe before I was raped had been challenging, but it was also often thrilling, and I was able to take genuine pleasure in the adventure. Traveling alone after the rape was simply grueling. Every day that I survived felt like an accomplishment, which I suppose was a good thing, or at least better than it feeling like a failure, but it was as if I was at boot camp and not on vacation. Still, I pushed through, moving from one bad choice to another, caught in a pattern of unconscious re-enactment with little hope of deflating the power of the emotional triggers that gripped me.

I found a job pulling pints at the Phene Arms, a pub in Chelsea just five minutes south of the King's Road off Oakley Street (the pub closed down a number of years ago, shortly after the death of its most famous patron, iconic footballer George Best). I found a room in a flat above another pub, which was five minutes directly north where Oakley meets the King's Road. I had worked at the Phene Arms for about six weeks before my boyfriend arrived. My most vivid memory of this time is of my nightly walk home from one pub to the other, along one dark and leafy brownstone-lined street of upper-class Chelsea and up another. The stress of this walk was incapacitating, but I felt like I had no other way to get home. There was no public transportation to take you across side streets, and it wasn't possible to just hail a cab—besides, taxis in London were prohibitively expensive, especially on my student budget. What's more, I felt stupid and embarrassed about how skittish this short walk made me. This was upper-class London, after all; what could possibly happen to me?

I tried to make myself feel safe by walking in the center of the deserted streets and humming aloud. I also bought a personal keychain alarm, which I wore around my neck, and which was set off by releasing the key from the unit. I walked at a fast clip holding the key, peering back and forth, over one shoulder and then the other. It was ridiculous. The rape was four years behind me, and Robert Dinges had been sentenced to eight years in jail. But that was cold comfort, and my body knew it. And so I found myself, night after night, retracing the steps of my vulnerability down the posh streets of Chelsea.

3: Live In It

In the summer of 1996, after finishing my MA in philosophy at the University of Manitoba, I moved to Toronto with my boyfriend. We both had been accepted into the PhD program in philosophy at the University of Toronto, and we were preparing to start there together in the fall. By then, six years had passed since the rape, and outside of a couple of sessions with a psychologist when I first returned home from Paris (attended at the behest of my parents), I had made no serious effort to come to terms with the experience. I believed—wrongly, as it turns out—that the best way to deal with the trauma of that night was to distance myself from it. I had stopped thinking about it and talking about it and over time I had successfully managed to forget about it, or at least, suppress the experience from my everyday conscious thought. I was doing my best to just leave the ordeal behind me, but it was ineluctably tethered to me and, like any wound that goes untreated, the more I ignored it the worse things got. My relationship was in its final stages. The feeling of an imminent betrayal that plagued me throughout our years together was relentless, and five years on I still could not shake it. Despite my deep love and affection for my boyfriend, by the end of our relationship I had very little capacity for intimacy. I could not push through the emotional and psychological barriers that had built up between us.

Although this was not how I saw it at the time, it seems obvious to me now that my incapacity to trust, which shaped the tenor of that relationship, is best understood through the filter of my rape rather than as a response to my partner's infidelity. Although it was true that he had been unfaithful to me at the start of our relationship, the severity of my response was disproportionate to his actions. Even though we had umpteen moments of effortless, happy closeness, I was never able to sustain a feeling of security in the relationship. This is something I still struggle with, but I understand it better now. It is symptomatic of the catastrophic thinking that I referred to earlier, which is typical in those who suffer from PTSD and is characterized by a nervous system that is on high alert: fearing for the worst, and living in a constant expectation of harm. I would occasionally manage to overcome the feeling that my well being was at risk. I would let my guard down and settle into an easy pace only to be jolted back into a state of vigilance at the first sign of any dissonance in my life.

Things only got worse for me when that relationship ended. Since my first panic attack at Charles de Gaulle airport on August 2, 1990, I had been averaging three or four attacks a year, but now I was single and living alone in a relatively new city, and I was having three or four a *month*. Panic attacks can persist for hours, but in my case a typical one would last for less than five minutes. The anxiety would come on me, seemingly without warning, and suddenly I would be gripped by an intense feeling of terror for my physical safety, followed closely by an almost paralyzing fear that I might faint or lose control of my bodily functions. My heart would race out of control and the oxygen would drain out of the room. These attacks were exhausting, and I began to live in dread of them. I had been a smoker since my rebellious teenage years, and I used to believe (contrary to fact) that cigarettes helped to calm me down, so whenever I could I chain-smoked my way through the panic.

I had a whack of other problems as well, which had been more or less suppressed by the dynamics of my relationship, but they spilled out as soon as I no longer had that as a container for them. In the middle of the fall of 1997, a few months after the breakup, my breathing, which had been intermittently shallow since the rape, became perpetually so. I was jumpy; I had minor convulsions at the slightest unexpected noise, anything from the ringing of a telephone to the slamming shut of a book. My ability to fall and stay asleep, which had been a struggle since the rape, became seriously compromised. I would lie in bed for hours listening to the pounding of my own heart and trying to close off my mind to the unwanted images that flew threw it. These intrusive thoughts are a form of traumatic flashback, although since I wasn't actually thinking (or writing or talking) about the rape at that time in my life, these images weren't usually about me or Robert or the knife grazing lines on my breasts. Instead, the intrusive thoughts were centered on my friends and family, and every possible variation that my mind could configure on each one's violent and imminent demise. In quick, successive flashes, I would imagine one sister or the other trampled by the crush of an uncontrollable

mob, or my grandmother's head ripped off by a bus whiz-
zing past her, or a friend flattened to death by a crash-
ing plane. At the time, alcohol was the only thing that
gave me some temporary relief from these tormenting
thoughts, and even though I was a relatively poor grad
student I began to cultivate a predilection for single-malt
scotch. I would bring a bottle of the stuff into my bedroom and drink myself to sleep to dull the force of these
images, only to relive them again in my dreams.

To complicate matters, I kept the details of my disastrous inner life to myself. I mentioned to my family and
a couple of my closest friends that I was having some
anxiety, but I was too ashamed to disclose the full extent of my problems. By then I had been hemmed in by
feelings of shame for so long that the sense of discon-
nection those feelings created between my private and
public self felt normal. Shame is an emotion that many
rape survivors struggle with for reasons that can be more
complicated than we might think. It is a distinctly insidious form of humiliation, the result of a serious injury to
our self-esteem, which can be exacerbated by the feeling that we've done something wrong. Humiliation is par
for the course when your body is used sexually against
your will—that part of the aftermath of sexual violence
is pretty well understood. Less well appreciated is why
rape survivors may end up feeling responsible for what
has happened to them. A common assumption is that
women blame themselves because of low self-esteem:
if only I had dressed differently, if only I had not looked
at him that way, if only I had made better decisions for
myself. While a woman's self-image may play a role in
how she comes to understand what has happened to her,

the sense of responsibility held by many rape survivors is at least partly driven by a dominant worldview regarding personal safety and harm. Although this picture is slowly changing, historically, at least in the West, girls have been taught from a young age that the world is basically a safe place and that so long as you are sufficiently careful and intelligent, you can protect yourself from any serious harm.

Underscoring this narrative is the fact that in our entertainment-saturated media culture, the everydayness of sexual violence against women is overlooked in favor of sensationalized stories of extreme violence. And because rape is typically experienced in private, unlike other traumatic experiences, like combat fighting in war, for instance, the clear evidence of its pervasiveness is obscured from our collective vision. This further reinforces the mistaken notion that the world is a benign place for women—and worse, it makes incidents of sexual violence against women look like a series of unrelated, isolated events when in fact they are the systematic consequence of patriarchal social structures.

So how does the rape survivor reconcile this dominant worldview with what has happened to her? After all, it cannot be true both that the world is a safe place and that you were raped, unless, of course, the rape was your fault. The other alternative is to reject the dominant worldview, but this means accepting the fact that we live in a world where women, by virtue of being women, are at risk. For a variety of reasons, it can be easier and less painful to believe instead that being raped was a result of your own poor choices.

*

Shame is a corrosive and insidious emotion, and the shame that engulfed me after my rape was exacerbated by one particularly bad decision that I made immediately following the experience, when I got back home to Winnipeg. One of the first issues that I had to deal with was what I was going to tell people about what had happened to me. My summer in Europe had been cut short by two weeks, and it would have been difficult for me to hide that fact from my friends, and also from certain family friends, whose kids had been traveling around Europe that summer with Lisa and me. I would need to give some explanation for my premature homecoming. I talked it over with my parents and together we fabricated a story that I told everyone in my life. The only people who knew the truth were my parents, my sisters, and my two closest friends, all of whom I swore to secrecy on pain of death. The details of the lie are now vague, but loosely, the story was that I had been robbed and pushed around a bit at knifepoint. Following the "mugging," left with minor bruises and no money, my zest for adventure had understandably disappeared and I decided to come home early.

It is easy to see now that the decision to cover up the rape was a mistake. It became a secret that festered inside of me like a malignant tumor, but at the time it seemed like the right thing to do. The decision came out of a long discussion I had with my parents on August 2, the night I returned home from Paris. I wasn't exactly in my right mind. The combination of shock, lack of sleep, and physical pain had left me wired, but I wanted to talk. I needed to try to get my head around the fact that I had just been raped. At some point during this discussion I wondered aloud whether in some way I had been responsible for what had happened to me, but my parents quickly dismissed that possibility and, with only a bit of a false note, I concurred. On some level I knew that they were right and so I ignored the bubbling suspicion I had to the contrary. But I remember feeling at the time that I was overcompensating. I also remember launching into a monologue about the vulnerability of women in male-dominated societies. I was fresh out of my first women's studies course at the University of Manitoba, and while I lacked any understanding of the neurobiological and psychological damage of rape on a survivor, I had some sense of the politics of sexual violence; in an instant I intellectualized what had happened to me. Just one day after I was raped I was engaging in a theoretical discussion with my parents about the structural causes of rape in a patriarchal society. I even remember hearing myself (again with only a bit of a false note) telling them that rape wasn't about sex, but about power, which might be an accurate way to characterize certain unconscious motivations of a rapist, but is a thoroughly inaccurate characterization of what rape is for a rape survivor, whose relationship with sex and her own body may be changed forever. In any case, we agreed that Robert Dinges was a lunatic and that I had been in the wrong place at the wrong time. They also blamed Stream and Roditi, and initially, at least, I did too. And while we agreed that it had not been my fault that I had been raped, I was simply in no position to go public with the events of the previous night. Just thinking about telling my story to others made me feel unbearably exposed, and so together my parents and I decided that it would be easiest on me if we instead kept the truth to ourselves.

Although my position then was that I wanted to keep the rape private because of how hard it would have been on me to tell (and retell) my story, I can see now that that was, at best, only partly true. I was vulnerable, fragile, and already profoundly embarrassed by my bad luck. Whether or not I was responsible for what had happened to me, I was hot with shame over it. And while maybe I could convince myself that I had done nothing wrong, I could not predict how others might react, and frankly, I was too messed up to risk finding out. I was confused, literally unable to think straight. Overnight my identity had changed. I was suddenly a "rape survivor." I was stunned by this new sense of self and completely at a loss for how to assimilate it. And, unfortunately, I didn't have the kind of support that I needed to help me come to what would have been in the long run a better decision. It is not that my parents weren't supportive—they most certainly were—but their efforts were focused on shielding me from anything that might cause me further pain. I took the lead and my parents, with the best intentions, helped me to disguise my blistering raw vulnerability with a lie. None of us knew that the choice to keep the rape a secret would ultimately make things harder on me.

Whether to go public with her story is one of the toughest decisions a rape survivor faces, for all the reasons just mentioned—the vulnerability, the shame, the embarrassment, and the inescapable feeling that she should have been able to prevent herself from being attacked, and then some—all reinforced by the myth that, so long as you are careful, the world is a safe place. Rape intersects with multiple taboos—sex, violence, and trauma—and its savage intrusion on our sexuality crosses the boundary into that which is most personal and private. For all these reasons, it is simply not socially acceptable for a woman to speak out about her experience as a rape survivor. This taboo is more deeply ingrained in cultural norms in certain parts of the world, like south-central and eastern Asia, Africa, and the Middle East, where the survivor's shame extends to her entire family, often permanently, and where the consequences for women who publicly identify as rape survivors can be disastrous, even fatal. But even in the West, outside of therapists' offices and certain professional contexts, talking about one's personal experience with sexual violence is universally off-limits.

This amounts to a lot of pressure on survivors to stay silent, and it is easy to see why women fold under the weight of it all. Still, hiding the truth about our individual experiences with sexual violence can be problematic. Keeping our rape stories secret lowers the decibel level on the magnitude of the problem and perpetuates the idea that rape happens somewhere else, to someone else. It makes us complicit in the act of covering up the realities of sexual violence against women, which helps to preserve the myth that women have complete control over their bodies. Again, the picture of rape that falls out of this worldview turns rape into a personal problem rather than a social one. No wonder rape survivors end up blaming themselves.

Perhaps even more importantly, there can be a tremendous cost to individuals who bury their experience and carry it as a secret. This can accentuate the shame they struggle against and open a chasm between their private

selves; their emotional, physiological, and psychological realities; and their public personas—between who
we are and how others see us. At least that was my experience, and six years after the rape I was living a kind
of double life. On the one hand, I was a relatively high-
functioning grad student, working on my PhD in philosophy, winning sought-after grants and performing well,
at least academically. On the other hand, I ignored those
aspects of my body and mind that had been crippled by
the rape so completely that I was not even aware that my
turbulent inner life was connected to the trauma of the
rape. And because I was not yet fluent in the language of
PTSD, I did not know that what I was experiencing was
the manifestation of a cluster of symptoms typical among
rape survivors.

*

The history of posttraumatic stress disorder is a fascinating one. PTSD became an official psychiatric disorder
only recently, in 1980, with the publication of the third
edition of the American Psychiatric Association's hand-
book of mental disorders, the *Diagnostic and Statistical
Manual of Mental Disorders (DSM)*. For over fifty years
the *DSM* has been the bible for psychiatric care in North
America and elsewhere. Although it is the reigning authority on mental illness, it is not without its critics, who
worry about the clustering of symptoms as a way of iden-
tifying disorders, the proliferation of new diagnoses, and
the lowering of diagnostic thresholds (to name but a few
recent controversies). The roots of PTSD can be tracked
through the publication of the various editions of the
DSM, starting with the first edition, *DSM I*, in 1952, but

the history of the concept of psychological trauma goes back further than that.

Today, we use the word "trauma" when we talk about psychological scars, but the concept was once strictly reserved for physical wounds (this use is still found in expressions like "trauma wards" and "trauma surgeons"). Historians date the psychologization of the term to about the mid-nineteenth century, when, in the 1860s, the British physician John E. Erichsen diagnosed "railway spine" as a nervous disorder. Railway spine was a curious phenomenon in which an individual who had experienced the shock of a violent rail-car crash appeared to escape physically intact, but over time developed an impaired nervous system, exhibiting symptoms of irritability, loss of memory, numbing, and local paralysis. The absence of any detectable organic injury generated controversy among the leading scientists of the day over the primary cause of railway spine, and even Erichsen was equivocal on the matter: was railway spine caused by an undetectable spinal concussion, or did it originate in a psychological response to the sudden terror of a railway crash?

This debate over the main cause of railway spine opened the door to the idea of psychological trauma. The central figures in the development of the concept were the Parisian neuropsychiatrist Jean-Martin Charcot, who had a special interest in the neurological basis of "traumatic hysteria," and his onetime students, Pierre Janet (whose doctoral dissertation on *Psychological Automatism* [1889] has been singled out as the first systematic treatise on psychological trauma as the cause of hysteria) and Sigmund Freud, who popularized the concept.

At the end of the nineteenth century Freud published a number of papers on the traumatic origins of neuroses, including his coauthored study with Josef Breuer, *Studies on Hysteria* (1895). But it was in his paper "The Aetiology of Hysteria," first delivered in a public address to his colleagues in 1896, that made famous the view that the cause of hysteria (or neurosis) in adults could be traced back to sexual "seduction" in childhood. This view, known later as Freud's seduction theory, took as fact the claims of his female patients that something terrible and violent had occurred in their pasts. Childhood sexual traumas, which had been dismissed by other psychiatrists as the delusions of hysterical women, were now seen as real, cruel, and forced on the young children who suffered them. In a number of papers written in 1896, early childhood sexual abuse was cited by Freud as the cause of damaging and lasting neuroses in adults.

In 1905, less than ten years after putting forward this theory on the traumatic origins of neurosis, Freud notoriously retracted it (having already denounced it in private correspondence as early as 1897). Scholars disagree on why Freud changed his mind, and over the degree to which he truly did. Maybe Freud decided that he lacked good clinical support for his theory, or maybe he doubted the veracity of his patients (in a work published in the 1930s, Freud claimed that the tales of "seduction" by his female patients had been, in fact, mere fantasies). Or maybe, as some have suggested, the professional cost of implicating fathers of child abuse in the Victorian era was simply too high. Whatever his reasons were, when the seduction theory disappeared from the headlines so did any interest in the traumatic origins of neuroses, at least for the time being.

The debates were revived in the 1920s, with the almost epidemic appearance of what was then called "shell shock," a popular diagnosis for the anxiety-like symptoms exhibited by soldiers during World War I. As a sound diagnostic category, however, shell shock was controversial. At the time, there were military leaders and physicians who disputed its legitimacy and argued that shell shock was a combination of cowardice and malingering—an affliction of the weak. As a diagnosis for individuals suffering from the effects of terrorizing life events, psychological trauma fell in and out of favor throughout the twentieth century, disappearing for decades and then reappearing again in the early 1970s, largely as a result of a fight being waged by Vietnam War activists, both veterans and psychiatric workers, on behalf of those suffering from war-related trauma.

This recent history of posttraumatic stress can be traced through the various editions of the *DSM*. In the *DSM I*, for instance, the entry for "gross stress reaction" described it as a temporary condition that was produced by extreme environmental stress, which should disappear after the individuals are removed from the stressful situation. The *DSM II* (1968) contained a number of new kinds of mental illnesses and eliminated others, including gross stress reaction. Some have speculated that the absence of any specific psychiatric disorder produced by combat in this edition was due to the fact that those writing the *DSM II* had no firsthand experience with "war neurosis" from either World War II or the Korean War.

It was not until the publication of the *DSM III* in 1980 that posttraumatic stress disorder entered the medical nomenclature as a psychiatric category. The story of how PTSD ended up in the manual is essentially a political one, and it was set in motion around the late 1960s, at the peak of the U.S. involvement in the Vietnam War. Vietnam War veterans were beginning to organize to protest against the war, and they started to hold "rap groups," informal gatherings where veterans talked openly about their war experiences, in various cities across the United States. The New York chapter of one of these groups invited two prominent antiwar psychiatrists, Chaim Shatan and Robert Lifton, to sit in on some sessions, apparently more as allies against the war than as medical health professionals. Shatan and Lifton observed among the veterans what they called "delayed massive trauma," which manifested symptoms of guilt, rage, psychic numbing, and alienation. Along with other war activists, Lifton and Shatan were instrumental in bringing awareness to what they perceived as the psychiatric problems associated with psychological trauma. In May 1972, the *New York Times* published an article by Shatan titled "The Post-Vietnam Syndrome," and the die was cast for what has since been dubbed "the *DSM III* revolution"—the fight to get PTSD included in the third edition of the *DSM*. It was not long after that feminists began to notice that the kinds of symptoms associated with war-related traumas were widespread among women and children who had suffered from rape and other forms of domestic and sexual violence, and they too joined in the effort to get official recognition for PTSD. Over seventy years after Freud had suggested that traumatic symptoms in adult women were due to early childhood sexual abuse, in the midst of the second wave of the women's movement in North America, the idea had finally taken root. Nowadays, sexual violence is widely regarded as one of the most common causes of PTSD.

*

When PTSD appeared in the *DSM III* it was classified as an anxiety disorder and defined by the development of certain characteristic symptoms that follow exposure to a traumatic stressor. PTSD is notable among mental disorders in having an environmental event as part of its diagnostic criteria, but in the *DSM III* the criterion for a traumatic stressor was vague, stating only that "it would evoke symptoms of distress in almost everyone." This criterion was amended in the revised *DSM III-R* (1987), which defined a traumatic event as something "outside the range of usual human experience" and offered examples of qualifying events, "such as a serious threat to life or physical integrity." The problem with this characterization, however, is that if "usual" is understood statistically, as in an average experience, then the requirement that the traumatic stressor fall outside the range of a usual human experience is false, since serious threats to life and physical integrity like rape and war are common. As a result, this descriptor was dropped in later editions, but the challenge of coming up with a sufficiently specific conceptualization of a traumatic stressor has remained in all subsequent editions of the *DSM*, and is one reason why PTSD continues to be one of the most controversial entries in the *DSM*.

For instance, in the fourth edition of the *DSM*, published in 1994, the scope of experiences that could count as traumatic stressors was broadened to include observing or receiving information about the traumatic events suffered by others. One advantage of this way of understanding a stressor is that the range of people who can legitimately be said to be suffering from PTSD-related symptoms includes those who work in law enforcement, for example, or judges in a criminal court—individuals who by virtue of their jobs are required to hear and observe case after case (or scene after scene) of violent imagery.

But the expansion of the category of traumatic stressors also raises concerns. It allows for the possibility, for instance, that someone who watched, on television, planes crash into the Twin Towers on 9/11 could be equally traumatized as someone who managed to escape from one of the falling buildings, which, if not obviously false, is at least counterintuitive. This problem has been partly resolved in the recently published *DSM 5* (2013), which limits exposure to the traumatic events of others through electronic media, television, movies, or pictures to that which is work-related. But the stressor criterion in the *DSM 5* allows for indirect exposure in other ways, namely through learning of violent or accidental traumatic events that happen to close family members or friends.

One problem with the ongoing expansion of the criterion of a traumatic stressor is that we risk further diluting what is arguably the most overused and misapplied label in psychiatric medicine. Colloquially, we use expressions like "how distressing" and "how upsetting" interchangeably with "how traumatic," which can be seen as a trickle-down effect from the growth in popularity of PTSD as a diagnosis for all manner of difficult life events. If now just hearing about someone else's traumatic experience can be traumatic, we may have a hard time distinguishing a genuinely traumatic event from one that, though very distressing, is not psychologically jolting. Underscoring this problem is the unassailable connection between science and politics. War veterans and others whose jobs put them in life-threatening situations and who develop PTSD as a result are remunerated for their suffering. But because claiming to have PTSD can be lucrative, there are skeptical worries about less-than-honest motives at work in the classification of what counts as a traumatic stressor.

But the real worry here is that we may end up pathologizing people's normal reactions to upsetting life events, thereby creating medical conditions out of routine distress. This is a criticism that one hears a lot about the *DSM*, and the proliferation, with each new edition, of all manner of anxiety and depressive disorders. Is shyness one among many normal responses to being in a social setting, for instance, or is it a symptom of "social phobia disorder"? Is deep yearning and prolonged sorrow after the death of a loved one a normal response to grief or a sign of "persistent complex bereavement disorder"?

The diagnostic categories that crop up in each new edition of the *DSM* raise bona fide concerns about whether these are cases of real, neurobiological disorders or socially constructed ones. In the case of PTSD and other mental disorders that seem to reach epidemic proportions, there is a further concern about overdiagnosis. Are the diagnostic thresholds for certain mental disorders set too low? This question is particularly pressing in the case of PTSD. We want to make sure that we do not mistake a normal response to a shocking event for a psychiatric illness. Having some anxiety or depression after hearing about someone else's traumatic experience is normal. It is both a common experience and an appropriate response. Having anxiety, depression, or even panic after experiencing firsthand a traumatic event is also normal. But in cases where the symptoms take on a life of their own, and when they are severe and persistent, then the response becomes pathological. In other words, it is only when individuals are unable to recover from the natural distress that follows the experience of a traumatic event that, by our current mental health standards, their symptoms are indicative of a mental disorder.

*

In the *DSM III* and the *DSM IV*, PTSD symptoms are classified into three main clusters: intrusive recollection/reexperiencing, avoidant/numbing, and increased arousal. In the *DSM 5*, numbing symptoms have been moved to a fourth cluster: negative alterations in mood/cognition. There is a handful of different sorts of manifestations of each cluster. One might reexperience the traumatic event, for instance, through intrusive thoughts, recurrent distressing dreams, flashbacks, involuntary memories, and psychological distress and physiological reactions when faced with triggers of the event. Avoidant symptoms include avoidance of external reminders of the experience and of any thoughts and memories connected to it. Negative mood and cognitions include diminished interest, feeling negatively about oneself, feeling detached and estranged from others, and blocking out distressing memories due to dissociative amnesia. Hyperarousal symptoms include difficulty falling or staying asleep, difficulty concentrating, irritability, an exaggerated startle response, and hypervigilance. If you have a significant cross section of these symptoms that persist over time and are preceded by a traumatic stressor, then, according to current best practices, you have PTSD.

My symptoms were textbook. The intrusive thoughts and dreams, the catastrophic thinking, the sleep problems, the avoidance and detached feelings, the shallow breathing and panic, the jumpiness—each one a classic symptom of posttraumatic stress disorder, but in the fall of 1997 I was oblivious to this fact. My relationship with the guy who I had never been able to trust had just ended, and I thought that my near-crippling anxiety was due to the fallout of the breakup of that relationship. Still, as the months wore on I became increasingly incapacitated. I had a hard time feeling safe, ever. As a result, I spent a lot of my time holed up in my apartment, but even locked up in there I felt in danger. My body was always on high alert. I would hear a noise in the hallway outside of my apartment, and I would tiptoe to my front door and squint out my peephole to check for potential intruders. I spent the winter hiding out, vexed by the onslaught of these paralyzing symptoms.

By the spring of 1998 I had finally had enough. I decided that I needed to get some help. I went to see a psychiatrist, which is how I first ended up on clonazepam. Remarkably, I saw this doctor once a month for about a year, and not once in that time did I mention to her that

I had been raped or almost killed. At the time I wasn't even aware of this omission (I realized it only after I went back to see her following a long hiatus). It wasn't that I had entirely blocked out any memory of the rape, but by this point I had assumed that it was long behind me, and I simply did not connect my wretched inner life with the aftermath of that traumatic experience. The event of August 1, 1990, had fallen off my radar even though I was living it out every day.

My psychiatrist put me on a twice-a-day dose of clo-nazepam, and after about a month my breathing returned to normal. The pills also helped my other PTSD-related symptoms. I began to sleep better, and my panic attacks subsided. For the next year or so I was able to focus on my studies and ignore the ebbing turmoil of my inner life. But in the spring of 1999, I got into another serious relationship and my psychic life blew up again. This rela-tionship had a clean beginning, yet all the emotions that had controlled me during my previous relationship came back in full force. The catastrophic thinking returned, as did my inability to trust and the familiar feeling of an im-pending betrayal, and this time I could not account for my mess of emotions by pointing to some infidelity on the part of my partner. I was dating a faithful and loving man, and I was insanely suspicious of him. And as these feelings worsened so did the awkward juxtaposition be-tween my public and private selves. My identity was split in ways that felt irreconcilable.

And then I began to have problems with sex—or rather, the problems that I had been having with sex became too much for me to handle. In the near-decade since the rape, my relationship with my body had grown into one of estrangement. It is often said that rape is about power and not sex, but as I suggested before, this can be a misleading characterization. It is true that power imbalances in society create the conditions that make it possible for men to rape, and it is also true that men may rape out of a desire not for sex but for absolute power and control over another person. But for the survivor, rape is all about sex. It is about having the most private parts of your body used sexually, violently, against your will. Like most survivors, this experience of forced sex insinuated itself into my sex life, in perpetuity, it seems, shadowing every intimate physical gesture, a persistent reminder that my body is not entirely my own.

*

The unremitting state of traumatic flashbacks that I endured during each sexual encounter in the first nine months following my rape was agonizing, but as I said before it came as an unexpected relief when I finally told my boyfriend about what had happened to me. Once he was aware of what triggered me during sex he was able to modify his behavior to help ease my flashbacks. Although we stopped seeing each other not long after the HIV scare, the experience taught me that sex could be a whole lot easier for me if my romantic partners knew my story.

When that relationship ended and I became involved my next boyfriend, I immediately had the same kinds of problems with sex. Before I told him that I had been raped I remained caught in traumatic memories each time we were physically intimate. I would have flashbacks, but also, in anticipation of the impending disclosure, I would play out the conversation in my mind, over and over again: "I need to tell you about something that happened to me," or, "But don't worry, you're not at risk, I'm not HIV-positive." For as long as these sentences stayed in my head they had a certain hold over me, and I knew that I had to say them out loud. But I kept putting off the conversation. It just seemed so heavy, compared to the levity of new love. I was worried about burdening the relationship and so I avoided telling him for as long as I could stand it. But finally, after a couple of months, I worked up the courage and told him my secret. Once again it was hard to get the words out, but it was worth it, because it meant that I no longer had to pretend around him.

This pattern repeated itself in the spring of 1999, as I entered into another long-term relationship, but this time the element of release that came from sharing my story was only temporary. In the previous years there had been days and months that had passed without any conscious thought about the rape, but I was now having sex again regularly, and despite the fact that it was often good in lots of ways, the rape was once again always present. Even though my new boyfriend knew about my various triggers and was tender and mindful of them, certain parts of my body remained intolerably sensitive to the touch—my neck, my head, my breasts, and my upper back. It became impossible for me to get lost in sex. There was always some touch or movement that brought me back to the night of August 1, 1990.

I became seriously inhibited, and despite the many pleasures of a new relationship I was not on the whole enjoying myself. I had reached a turning point. Forced into a corner, I had to admit that the problems that I had been experiencing in my intimate, sexual relationships were mine, and mine alone. I finally faced the niggling suspicion that I had been pushing aside for almost a decade and decided that it was time to find someone who could help me deal with the rape and its aftermath. I asked a friend who was in therapy for a recommendation, and I made a phone call that changed the course of my life and initiated the long process of recovery.

*

I have learned as much about the human condition from my therapist, Anique Rosenbaum, as I have from any philosopher I have ever studied. She has taught me about human psychology, freedom, and the elusive connections between mind and body. Through our work together I have learned a number of important lessons about the impact of psychologically traumatic experiences and about the process of recovering from them. One is that a traumatic experience is influential. Trauma changes us. Extreme stress affects brain functioning. It changes our physiology in ways that researchers can now literally see, thanks to advances in neuroimaging techniques. When a person's fight-or-flight instinct is interrupted, when the automatic impulse to resist or escape danger is impossible, our natural impulse to organize an effective response to threat fails and the human nervous system becomes overwhelmed, chaotic, and immobilized. This is what happens in traumatic experiences like rape, although in some cases individuals recover relatively easily.

Experts say that a person's response to a traumatic event hinges on her predisposition to anxiety and stress disorders, which, in turn, depends on a complex mix of genetic and environmental factors. Recent studies have suggested, for instance, that the presence of one of the two variations of the *COMT* gene (what's been called the "worrier" gene), which regulates the breakdown of dopamine to the brain, can be an important genetic indicator. But since it is very difficult to control for environmental influences in scientific studies, and since the ways that genes interact both with other genes and with the environment is unpredictable, it is hard to determine the significance of genes alone on the development of anxiety and stress disorders. What does seem clear, however, is that the combination of genetic and environmental factors in early childhood development has a major influence in determining a person's vulnerability to traumatic stress. Not everybody responds the same way to the same event. Mental health professionals have long believed that individuals are especially sensitive to adverse environmental influences early in life, obstacles like chronic poverty, physical or sexual abuse, or inappropriate care, and the current science supports this. Recent studies in developmental neurobiology confirm that our brains are particularly malleable in early development, and that the neural circuits that govern emotion and stress are shaped at this time. It seems safe to say that environmental conditions in early childhood development are responsible, at least in part, for the broad variation that we see in people's resiliency to the experience of traumatic stress.

What this suggests is that our susceptibility to psychological damage hinges on whether there is some preexisting vulnerability present in us, which is then triggered by a traumatic episode. In these cases, an incident of traumatic stress weakens one's resistance, the underlying condition is revealed, recovery is halted, and PTSD develops. When that happens, trauma etches a neurobiological change in people. Certain parts of the brain become atrophied as a result of trauma (the amygdala, hippocampus, and hypothalamus), and other parts are underutilized (there is a decreased activation of the medial prefrontal cortex).

Science helps to explain why trauma is influential. PTSD is a consequence of what happens when our biological response to threat—fight-or-flight—gets interrupted and frozen in a state of readiness. The result of this is a physiological disruption; our circuits go awry and our neurobiological systems—the systems that regulate sleeping, breathing, and talking—misfire and become maladapted. This is manifest in all the typical symptoms of PTSD, which get triggered when something in our environment reminds us (consciously or not) of the traumatic event. Our brains prompt our bodies to react not to anything in the here and now but to the paralyzing terror that overwhelmed us in the moment of the trauma. Again, this is what leads to the maladaptation—the numbing and the hyperarousal, the anxiety and the panic—all part of the physiological manifestations of what mental health professionals call the "inability to regulate affect." So, for instance, traumatized individuals tend to overreact (or underreact) to certain situations—they get too angry or not angry enough. They blow up in response to a slight provocation, or become incapacitated when frustrated. A lot of this behavior would have been appropriate at the time of the trauma, but outside of that context it is incongruous. So, on the face of it, the behaviors look irrational; indeed, in some sense they are *not* rational in that they are not reasoned responses.

When I hear a door slamming shut, my body jumps. It reacts automatically. The response is not deliberated or thought out in any way. It is not a cognitive response, but a complex physiological one, and what's clear is that these physiological responses do not always match our rational reflections. I might believe that I am perfectly safe in some given circumstance, for instance, but my body may nevertheless respond as if it were under threat. As I said earlier, our bodily responses to situations do not neatly track our beliefs about the world. And because these physiological reactions are not rooted in rational thought, no amount of rational persuasion can help to reason oneself out of them, as I discovered at the police station on the night I was raped, and again on that balmy New Year's morning in 1991, hanging out at Café Le Conti in Paris, and each time I got into my Honda Accord hatchback. What's more, the part of the brain that is connected with language (the left temporal lobe and cerebral cortex) is only peripherally related to the parts of the brain (again, the amygdala, hippocampus, and hypothalamus) that hold the imprint of the trauma, which further helps to explain why in moments of high anxiety it is hard to talk oneself out of feeling a certain way. But if reasoning about one's behavior cannot override it, then recovery from a traumatic experience must be rooted in something else.

If trauma results in deep neurobiological changes in people, how do we correct for that? How do individuals recover from terrifying life events over which they have no control? Back in 1999, the only thing I was sure of was what the answer to that question was not: ignore it. And so, with the guidance of my therapist, I began to process the trauma of the rape. It took me one session to tell Anique the story about what happened to me on the night of August 1, 1990, and many years of weekly therapy sessions to start to process it. It was through my work in therapy that I learned what I take to be the single most important lesson about recovery from traumatic events, which is that in order to break free from the hold of the memory of a traumatic experience you have to first *live in it*. Our biological instincts get jammed during a traumatic event, our motor system is interrupted, and we are prevented from taking care of ourselves in an appropriate way. Some theorists argue that the fact that we get stuck in this way means that we are literally unable to experience the traumatic event as it is happening to us. We may survive and move on in our lives, but, at some level, our bodies don't know that we are out of danger. The body, as it has been said, remembers. The body keeps score, and this is why the event returns against our will, haunting us in our dreams, intrusive thoughts, and other forms of flashbacks. Because traumatic experiences get held in our bodies, in order to digest the imprint of the trauma we need to consciously revisit the memory of the experience and move through it, thereby essentially retraining our neurological and physiological responses.

Plausibly, there are a number of different ways of accomplishing this, though most presuppose some form of neuroplasticity, a relatively new idea about how the brain changes itself through activity and thought, thereby allowing us to rewire our misfiring neural connections.

Individual psychotherapy is one way to do this, one that is often supplemented by group therapy and medication. Meds can help soften the severity of symptoms, which is what they did for me, and for this reason they can play an integral role in the recovery process. But, at least in my case, medication alone was not enough to rewire my misfiring neurotransmitters. For that, I needed to feel the full range of emotional and physiological responses that I was prevented from experiencing on the night of the rape, and I did this through my work with Anique, which was a form of psychotherapy. Psychotherapy, sometimes known as "talk therapy," often begins with narrative expression, but the process is not necessarily analytical, or based in forms of reasoning. Its practitioners are widely varied in their methods, so one has to be careful about making generalizations, but certainly there is a school of practice in which language is combined with sensation and movement to help individuals access their deeply felt emotional and bodily responses to traumatizing or otherwise influential life events. This method is sometimes called somatic psychotherapy. It was the approach that I undertook with Anique and it was incomparably hard.

The process passed through a number of different stages. It started with me sitting on Anique's couch, describing in detail everything about the night of the rape, about my rapist, and about the nine years that had passed since. With her insight I began to understand more and more about psychological trauma, and I began to grasp some of the reasons for the discrepancy between my beliefs about my personal safety and my bodily and emotional responses to triggering scenarios. As time went on and I felt increasingly safe in the environment that she had created for me, I went from sitting on the couch to lying down (the position I still take today), and then the really hard work began. Session after session I revisited the memory of August 1, but I was no longer analyzing it, or talking about it. Instead I let it take over my body. Anique helped me to stay grounded; she reminded me that I was in her office, in Toronto, in a safe place, and I closed my eyes while she guided me back to the night of the rape.

There were times when I felt the terror so vividly that it was as if I were back in Roditi's apartment on boulevard Massena, except that I wasn't. There was no knife scratching at my neck; instead there was someone gently coaching me, giving me permission to say all the things that I needed to say that night but couldn't. It was not easy work. With my eyes closed and the memories of that night in full color I often felt suffocated, lying there, as if Robert were still on top of me, not letting me move. The feeling was at times too much, and I would have to shake my legs and arms to pull myself out of it. At first, I had a tough time talking in this state. It was like I was trapped in the memories of the night, and I found it very hard to break the silence that Robert had imposed on me. But eventually I managed to find my voice, and when I did I told Robert to fuck off, over and over again. I told him that I hated him and that he had ruined my life, that he had ruined my body. In the safety of Anique's office I said things to him that I didn't even mean, like that I wished that he were dead, because the point of the exercise was to freely express my emotions and not to let reason interfere. In truth, I did not want him dead (nor did I want to chop off his penis, though that too was a common enough theme), but expressing these feelings was like a breath of fresh air.

After a period of time on the couch Anique and I agreed that I was ready to take this work to a new level, so she booked us into the first of many two-hour sessions at a local trauma resource center, a place that tries to create a private and safe space for survivors of physical and sexual violence to physically move around in so that they can scream and throw punches into the air. Trauma centers like this one offer the promise, however belated, of an opportunity to fight back. The rooms are soundproof, the lights are on dimmers, and each room has a supply of props, including gym mats and boxing gloves.

The notion that physical movement is important, even necessary, to the healing process is grounded in certain current theories about the way that trauma metabolizes in our brains and bodies. Talk therapy can be paramount in helping us understand things, and in the absence of understanding we can be held prisoners by our unconscious motivations. But understanding does not always facilitate change. Indeed, some experts reject the "talking cure" as an antidote to trauma. They agree that our neural connections can be rewired, but they argue that since it is physical helplessness that causes the nervous system to become disorganized in the first place, only physical movement can really help the brain to heal because only physical movement can reactivate those circuits that get caught in the moment of trauma.

Others go further and claim that since traumatic memories are written into the body, these memories are inaccessible by talk therapies. This way of thinking has led to an emphasis on body-oriented therapies, including a variety of sensorimotor and somatic psychotherapies, which aim to process trauma by changing core physiological states, as well as nonstandard somatic therapies, like yoga, meditation, and martial arts.

We know that traumatic experiences have a profound impact on our nervous system and sensorimotor reactions. Body-oriented therapies take seriously the idea that our past experiences are held in our present physiological states. There are different kinds of somatic therapies but the general idea behind them is that by moving your body around you trick your brain into passing through the state of readiness where it has been stuck, and in doing so you reorient yourself toward danger, thereby giving you greater control over your own nervous system.

But this is not quick work. It has been said that the brain never goes backward. According to experts, the neurobiological damage that results from terrorizing life events over which we have no control cannot be erased, and if posttraumatic stress is allowed to set in through years of emotional and physiological dysregulation, as it did in my case, it can take years of therapeutic activity to result in a brain whose default mode is not maladaptive.

Since at least as far back as Plato, philosophers have been preoccupied with the relationship between the mind and body. Is the mind part of the body, or the body part of the mind? Or are they distinct, and if so, how do they interact? Which of the two is in charge? I am not convinced that the science of trauma sheds new light on these philosophical questions, which seem to me as intractable as ever, but I can certainly vouch for the effectiveness of using the body to ease the mind. My sessions at the trauma center were intense. We would dim the lights and I would again close my eyes and revisit the memory of the trauma, but this time with boxing gloves on. I would try to free my mind of distraction and persuade it to return to a time and a place where I had been in danger.

These sessions were two hours long, and it usually took me about half of that time before I felt safe enough to move about in these body memories. Sometimes I would lie on my back and return to the moment when Robert was draped on top of me, raping me vaginally. My body would be tight in these instances, constricted by the weight of the image. But eventually I would find my strength and then I would push him off of me, with all the force of my bent arms and legs, again and again and again. Other times we set up gym mats against a wall, and I would stand in front of them with the intention of hitting them, of striking back as if it were Robert standing there. This was slow work, but eventually I became adept at throwing punches, and then after a bit more time I was able to talk—even scream—while I pounded away at the memory of that night.

*

My parents were very supportive of the work that I was doing in therapy, even if they could not fully conceptualize it. But they backed me emotionally and financially, and I could not have managed without them. A couple of years into the process I had a phone conversation with my dad about it. I can't remember what exactly I was talking about, but I mentioned to him that there was some detail about the rape that I wished I could remember better, and he responded by offering to check his file on it. I was stunned. This was the first I had heard of it—he had a file? About my rape? Maybe I shouldn't have been surprised. My dad, ever the lawyer, is in the habit of keeping detailed files on everything, so why not this? Although the news caught me off guard I was eager to see what he had, but I had to wait until the next time that I went to Winnipeg for a visit, which was a couple of months away.

When I finally got my hands on the file I was amazed to discover that it was over two inches thick. It contained every single piece of correspondence and document relating to the rape, most of which I had not seen in over ten years. In addition to all the letters to and from various members of the judicial system in Paris, the file included a number of medical documents, photocopies of airline tickets and hotel bills, and bank statements. There was also an official copy of the pretrial *indictment* from the cour d'appel in Paris, which contained my pretrial testimony and Robert's order for arrest, as well as a copy of the trial *judgment* from the cour d'assises.

After briefly glancing through the file with my dad I poured myself a few inches of his good scotch, retreated alone to my bedroom, and began to read. It took me hours to sort through the file, and what I found in it was unsettling. Each new letter elicited a memory—the names of the prosecutor and magistrate that I had dealt with over those first couple of years (Monsieur Thin, Madame Foulon), receipts of expenses from my two trips to Paris, business cards from the Hôtel Saint André des Arts, registered mail from the Royal Canadian Mounted Police (which had been hand delivered to me by a female officer whose job seemed to be to check in and make sure that I was alright and had proper support). There were letters to and from the Parisian lawyer we had worked with and a couple of official-looking letters from the Canadian Embassy in Paris. There were also two documents in the file that I did not remember ever having seen before. One was a five-page medical document dated May 27, 1991, in English, which showed the results from Robert's HIV test, which were straightforward enough, and which also contained the results from a psychiatric test. There were about ten points of conclusion drawn from this test, including the claim that Robert did not have "mental abnormalities of psychotic register," that he "did not find himself in a state of insanity at the time of the facts," and that "he is capable of being punished." It also concluded that "the alcoholism and the toximanic dependence as well as the search for different sensations are the origin of the commission of the offence." Different sensations? Different than what?

This information was off-putting, but then I came to the last page of the document where I found another set of conclusions that made reference to his blood type (which is A) and mine (which is O). There were also other details about various "secretions" and sperm that were found on the "brief under the seal," which obviously meant my underwear, which was when it first dawned on me that I must have gone to a hospital on the night of the rape. Of course, this made perfect sense. In most parts of the world it is standard protocol following any form of sexual attack. I would have seen a doctor or a nurse and had a rape kit performed. Sure enough, there was proof of this in the file, which contained two documents from the Hôtel-Dieu de

Paris dated August 1, 1990, that set out the *prescriptions pour victimes de Violences sexuelles* (such as being tested for HIV three months following exposure). What was disconcerting about this information was that I simply had no memory of going to a hospital. To this day, I have no memory of going anywhere but to the police station on the night of the attack, although I did remember walking around the station wearing, under my shorts, mesh underwear and a maxi pad, which I obviously had gotten at the hospital in exchange for my soiled underwear. But as I read through the rape file for the first time, the fact that I had gone to the hospital came to me as a surprise.

If this part of the sequence of events following the rape was vague in my memory, I could count on my dad to clear things up. Also in the file were five sheets of white notepad paper, stapled together, which were evidently his notes from my first phone call to him from the police station on the night of August 1. I might have been out of my mind during that call but my dad was sensible enough to write down a brief summary of my report to him, including the fact that when I called him I had already been with the police for an hour and a half, and that after the phone call I was "going to hospital." Whether I remembered it or not, there it was in his notes in the rape file, along with the blood analysis and medical documents from the Hôtel-Dieu, recorded at 3:30 p.m. Winnipeg time.

*

The nature and reliability of traumatic memories has been a matter of some debate since at least as far back as the late nineteenth century and the work of Janet, and Freud and Breuer. On the one hand, a traumatic event can be so startling that one's memories of it remain crystal clear for a lifetime. For instance, I will never forget the look on Robert's face as he traced the knife across my naked breasts—his demonic laughter, the distraction in his eyes. That image is seared into my brain for life. On the other hand, individuals have been known to dissociate in the face of an overwhelming life experience, which Janet referred to as a splitting (*dédoublement*) of the personality. This phenomenon is especially common in children and can be seen as a temporary adaptive mechanism, an unconscious ploy to help them survive a terrorizing life event that they lack the emotional and conceptual maturity to understand or process, let alone prevent. Take the example of a young girl whose dad routinely sneaks into her room at night and sexually abuses her. If the young girl is physically unable to escape the abuse then she can at least compartmentalize it and escape it in her mind, making it easier for her to have breakfast at the family table the next morning as if all were well (although this description makes dissociation sound more active and deliberate than it likely is). Still, our minds are powerfully protective of us and can trigger dissociation from horrific life events in order to help us to survive them and function through the daily routines of our lives.

All the evidence suggests that the extreme emotional cadence of trauma has contradictory effects on our memories—they can be detailed and vivid or fragmented and incomplete. Although the science of trauma has yet to uncover the answers to the mysteries around the complex processes of memory, one thing that is clear is that in moments of acute stress, the presence of high levels of emotion means that traumatic memories are shot with higher intensity than ordinary memories. Consequently, traumatic memories can be sharp and precise, but they can also be incomplete and disorganized. And it appears that in some cases the memory of a traumatic event can be forgotten altogether, or at least repressed, and held in our unconscious memory.

Occasionally dissociation happens during a traumatic event, like in the example above, where an individual disconnects from her body during a traumatic experience as a way of compartmentalizing it. Other times dissociation occurs in the aftermath of trauma, as part of the consequence of having an overwhelmed and jumbled neurobiological system. This is sometimes called "dissociative amnesia," or, more colloquially, "traumatic blocking." In cases like this the trauma survivor loses the capacity to integrate the memory of the traumatic event into what has been called the "declarative memory," that part of the memory that structures narratives, even if she continues to express aspects of the trauma behaviorally. In other words, the trauma survivor loses conscious hold on the details of the traumatic experience, even though she continues to experience it through flashbacks, intrusive thoughts, and other forms of somatic remembering. While dissociation can be temporarily adaptive, as in the case of the girl who blocks out the details of her abuse at the hands of her father in order to carve out a safe place for herself within her family home, the long-term effects are maladaptive. Dissociation can stunt healing by preventing the person from fully integrating the memories of a traumatic experience and structuring it into a coherent narrative.

*

The science of trauma has yet to reveal precisely how we encode, store, and retrieve traumatic memories. Certainly, the notion that our minds can repress traumatic memories was the subject of some controversy in the 1990s, with the emergence of "recovered memory syndrome," a phenomenon in which adults belatedly remember childhood sexual abuse, and its staunch opposition, "false memory syndrome," which calls into question the accuracy of recovered memories. While it might seem counterintuitive that we can forget something that should be imprinted in our memories forever, the way traumatic events are stored in the brain is simply not straightforward. As I looked through my rape file this was plain to me, since for the life of me I could not remember going to any hospital in Paris on the night of August 1, 1990. But then came an even greater shock. When I first scanned through the file there was a document that I had put aside and saved for last, the roughly ten-page English translation of the transcript of the pretrial *indictment*. It appeared to have been sent in September 1991 along with the original French version from the minister of justice in Paris to the minister of justice of Canada, in Ottawa, with a request that it be delivered to me at my parents' home via registered mail. I must have read it at the time, but it was now ten years later and I could not remember ever having seen it before. I had set it aside to read last not because I wanted to savor it, like icing on a piece of cake, but because I wanted to make sure that I had enough scotch in me before I got to it.

As I look through the transcript today I am fascinated by the details in it, which reveal, at least to my untrained mind, a sophisticated legal procedure. But mostly what I find interesting are the mundane facts about Robert: that he was born on February 11, 1960, in Betwiller, Bas-Rhin; that he is the son of Louis Dinges and of Dorothee Backi; that at the time he was caught he had no occupation; that his permanent residence was in Tours, in the home of Patricia Roland; and that he was first questioned in Nîmes on September 19, 1990, during an identity check. I was trembling when I read this for what felt like the first time, a decade after the rape. He had a birthday? Parents? He was born somewhere?

Most of this data could be found on the cover page of the document, following which is a full transcript of the *indictment*, which contains a record of my testimony of the event as told to the magistrate, Madame Sabine Foulon, in her office in January 1991. The first paragraph sets the scene on August 1, 1990, at about 9 p.m., when the police were called to intervene at 142 boulevard Massena, and then reverts back to earlier that day, around 5:30 p.m., when Stream came to pick me up at Gare du Nord. In plain language the transcript summarizes the sequence of events that took place after my arrival at Roditi's apartment up to the time that the police arrived. There was a description of Robert's threatening language; the knife; the oral, vaginal, and anal penetration; the knife scratches on my breasts; the cutting of the phone cord; and then the theft. I read through this all with a sense of detachment until I came to a paragraph that made my heart stop. It stated that after the theft "the accused again made the victim take her clothes off and forced her, still under threat, into further fellatio and anal penetration."

Remarkably, at some point during the course of the previous decade I had forgotten about this second round of violent penetrations. I had erased it from my memory, but, unlike the visit to the hospital, as soon as I read these lines the images of round two washed over me. I felt parched; I was stunned. I had been doing intensive work about the rape in therapy for close to two years by that point, yet somehow none of that had managed to jog this memory. I could not believe it. I had spent all that time on Anique's couch working through the memories of the rape, and yet I had failed to remember the dusty rose armchair.

It was terribly upsetting to discover that my memory of the rape was incomplete. I returned to Toronto with my rape file, which I brought to therapy for the next handful of sessions as I attempted to process these new pieces of information. I lay there week after week with the file on my lap, amazed that I had forgotten these key facts about the night. It is possible that the science of trauma will one day explain how it is that our brains block disturbing content from our conscious awareness. In the meantime, I tried to get my head around my repressed memories.

*

A traumatic experience impacts our physiology, our emotions, and our neurochemistry. It changes us. It can result in blocked memories, PTSD, and other forms of affect dysregulation—this is the influence of psychological trauma that I have been talking about. As my work in therapy progressed, however, I came to realize that there are two distinct sides to the aftermath of terrorizing life events. Traumatic events like rape can change our neurobiology, but they can also change the way we see ourselves, and our place in the world, by calling into question some of our core assumptions about our fellow human beings. Over the course of a marriage, a childhood, a date, or one hour, survivors of sexual violence learn certain odious facts about the possibilities of human behavior, and their worldview is shattered. Having suffered a traumatic experience, we might find ourselves forced, on pain of consistency, to give up some of our deeply held beliefs about human nature.

These are the twin sides of the aftermath of trauma. There is the shattered self, which is the influence of traumatic stress on our neurobiology, and the shattered worldview, which is its impact on our beliefs about the world. While all traumatic events are influential, they don't all result in a shattered worldview. Being in a car accident or suffering a natural disaster can be psychologically traumatic, but your view of the world does not necessarily change as a result. But when you are subjected to interpersonal violence your worldview is prone to change, because experiences like this teach us something about human nature. As I said before, in the West, at least, we are brought up to believe that the world is basically a safe place and that so long as we are dutifully careful we can protect ourselves from any serious harm. It is no wonder that we see ourselves as immune to acts of soul-crushing violence. Unfortunately, this is at best only partly true — that is, true only for adult men. Adult male rape certainly occurs, but outside of a prison environment it is statistically uncommon (for instance, Stream was in Roditi's apartment for days with Robert who, though clearly bisexual, made no attempt to rape him). The same cannot be said for the rest of the population. In every corner of the world adult women and young boys and girls are vulnerable to sexual violence. This violence can take different forms and it ranges in extremity, but insofar as it targets females it is part of a spectrum of oppression that is perpetuated by social structures of gender discrimination.

Unfortunately, this is a fact that individuals—indeed, whole societies—tend to cover up. There may be a number of good reasons for this. It could be that we mistakenly see sexual violence as a problem that happens elsewhere, in faraway countries and less developed places in the world, and not in our own backyards. It could be that we don't know the relevant facts, in other words. After all, the everydayness of sexual violence remains largely underground. The media are partly to blame for this; if it is not brutal or does not escalate into murder, then it is not newsworthy. But, as I once heard a journalist sadly remark about the routineness of domestic violence, there is simply no day on which it is news. Thus, unless we actively seek out this information, it can remain below our radar. Or perhaps we conceal the truth because we want to protect our children from the harsh realities of gender-based violence. One could argue that protecting children in this way as a means of instilling in them a robust sense of security is an important aspect of early childhood development. But at some point, sticking to this story becomes counterproductive, for as long as we are taught that the world is a benign place for women, when harm comes to us the most reasonable conclusion to draw is that it is our fault.

At the same time that I was grappling with my repressed memories I was struggling to come to terms with the bare fact of the everydayness of sexual violence and the shift in my worldview that this entailed. I began to shed my embarrassment around my own bad luck, and I began to accept that I was not invulnerable, which helped me to feel less ashamed for what had happened to me. But as I was coming to terms with this adjustment in my worldview I discovered a new challenge: how others reacted to it. This was around the summer of 2002, right around the time that I had started my new job at the University of Guelph. Because I had reached a stage in my recovery where I was feeling somewhat anchored, I made the decision to "come out" about the rape. I wanted those people close to me to know about this transformative event in my life. I wanted to reconcile my private life and my public persona. I wanted to finally tell my secret.

Initially, I came out about the experience by writing about sexual violence and PTSD in a couple of philosophical publications on sexual violence, where I self-identified as a rape survivor, but since not even other philosophers could be counted on to read those I could hardly expect my friends to find out that way. So, over the course of about six months I sat down with my friends and, one by one, told them my story. This was not easy. I had anxiety every time, but the hardest part about it was to see the pain and sadness in the faces of the people who cared about me. They were uniformly stunned by the details of the story and also by the fact that I had gone through something so monumental which they knew nothing about. Once the initial shock wore off, however, the important people in my life were entirely supportive. I felt incredibly lucky to have such good friends.

There was, however, one respect in which I felt occasionally misunderstood. I would find myself in a conversation with a friend, talking about how as a result of being raped I had come to understand that the world was not generally a safe place for women or children. I would talk about my shattered worldview and the heartbreaking statistics on sexual violence. And my interlocutor, with all the best intentions, would sympathetically assume that what I was trying to say was that I was feeling unsafe. In other words, my newly formed beliefs about the universality of gender-based violence and its place in a spectrum of oppressive behaviors toward women were interpreted not as statements of fact about the world, but as statements about me, and how well (or not) I was coping. I would patiently insist that the facts about violence against women had nothing to do with how scared or unsafe I was feeling at any given moment, but I found it hard to make myself heard on this point.

In the same way that our bodily responses to trauma do not always track our beliefs about the world, like when my heart pounds even when I believe that I am safe, our beliefs about the world do not neatly line up with our physiology. It is possible for a person to believe that she is at risk and yet not experience any fear or panic. So, for example, I might believe that skydiving is a dangerous sport and that once I jump out of an airplane there is a nonnegligible chance that I might not make it back to earth safely, and yet I might not feel any corresponding fear or panic as I am gliding freely through the air. Similarly, I might believe that I am not entirely safe right now, in my own home, as I type this sentence and yet not feel any corresponding alarm. I also may believe that men who are strangers to me can present a danger, yet not feel any fear in the presence of any particular man who is unknown to me. I might even accept the idea that the world is not an especially safe place for me as a woman and yet not live in a perpetual state of fear, having made the decision that there is little to be gained—and a good deal lost—by being always afraid. Indeed, I think it is fair to say that this is one of the main goals of psychotherapy: not to rid us of our beliefs about the world but to enable us to live well in spite of them.

As I told the story of my rape to my friends and acquaintances I felt loved and supported but occasionally misunderstood. I had a newfound awareness about the vulnerability faced by women and children worldwide, and my beliefs on the matter were substantiated not by my own experience but by the data on sexual violence, and yet not everybody took this view seriously. There were those who saw it as false and, more to the point, as corrupted and biased by my personal experience.

It could be that the denial of the harsh realities of sexual violence comes from a good place, a place of wanting to protect those people we love, and of wanting the world to be a different place. I understand these reasons, but as we have seen, the cost of accepting them is high.

*

When I began my work with Anique in 1999, my identity was split in ways that felt irreconcilable. Working with an exceptional therapist helped me to understand the impact of psychological trauma, to make sense of its profound influence on my body and mind. It taught me to recognize the psychological and neurobiological changes that result from terrorizing life events over which we have no control. Tracing my way back to the moment of the trauma and taking the time to live in it gave me the chance to start to retrain my nervous system and to push my body through where it had become stuck. Finally, I had begun to heal.

4: Africa, 2008

I had been teaching philosophy at the University of Guelph for six years when I was granted a sabbatical leave for the academic year 2008–2009. My plan was to use that time to start writing this book, and to prepare myself for this task I decided that I wanted to go to central Africa and see firsthand what I had come to understand as ground zero in the war against women. I had been following news of that continent through the writing of the award-winning journalist Stephanie Nolen, the Africa correspondent for the *Globe and Mail* from 2003 to 2008 and author of *28: Stories of AIDS in Africa*. Nolen's empathetic and insightful reporting had helped Canadians understand the complexity of some of the issues surrounding HIV/AIDS in Africa, and in her remarkable book she succeeded in putting a human face to the almost unfathomable scale of the problem. Nolen had helped shape my understanding of some of the cultural nuances of sexual violence against women and children in Africa, and of the way gender figured into the spread of HIV/AIDS. Between Nolen and Stephen Lewis—erstwhile statesman of Canadian leftist politics, former UN special envoy to Africa on HIV/AIDS, erudite author of the best-selling *Race Against Time*, and currently one of the world's foremost champions in the fight against HIV/AIDS—there was no mistaking that this was an epidemic of inequality.

Through the intricate layers of economics, politics, and geography, one picture remained clear in everything that I read about Africa: the heightened vulnerability of women and children on that continent. Rape was being used as a weapon of war in the Democratic Republic of the Congo; rape was being used as a strategy against refugees in any number of conflict zones; and, according to the myth that virgin blood is a panacea for disease and illness, infant rape and baby rape were being used as a cure for AIDS in South Africa and elsewhere. In war or peace, it seemed, women and children were at high risk. What's more, women and girls were the fastest growing demographic of people with HIV/AIDS in sub-Saharan Africa. UNAIDS, the Joint United Nations Programme on HIV/AIDS, has reported that in certain African countries, girls between the ages of fifteen and nineteen are six times more likely to be HIV-positive than boys of the same age. This is partly due to the widespread incidence of rape, but it can also be read as a sign of women's economic dependence on men, which makes it hard for them to negotiate appropriate sexual relations, including condom use, and boosts their reliance on transactional sex (the exchange of sex for money or material goods) for survival. The root of these problems in turn can be traced back to deep-seated structural inequalities between men and women.

Of course, problems associated with patriarchy are not exclusive to Africa. Gender discrimination and gender-based violence are universal. In Pakistan, estimates of women who suffer from spousal abuse range from 70 to 90 percent. In India, more than two-thirds of married women between the ages of fifteen and forty-nine have been beaten, raped, or otherwise forced to provide sex. Studies show that 50 percent of married Arab women are beaten at least once a year. And while rape is endemic in certain parts of Africa, the Middle East, and south-central and eastern Asia, the culture of rape in North America, where women are twice as likely to be raped as they are to get breast cancer, is hardly less appalling. In the United States, where there is a reported rape every six minutes, 17 percent of women have survived a completed or attempted rape. Of these, 21 percent were younger than twelve when they were first raped, and 32 percent were between the ages of twelve and seventeen. In Canada, half of the female population (51 percent) has experienced at least one incident of physical or sexual violence since the age of sixteen, and each week, one to two women are murdered by a current or former partner. And the situation is much worse in aboriginal communities in Canada, where some women undergo a lifetime of battering and sexual violence and are five to seven times more likely than non-aboriginal women to die as a result of violence. Statistics tell us that worldwide, one out of every three women will be beaten, coerced into sex, or otherwise abused in her lifetime. Pick almost any country in the world, East or West, rich or poor, and you can be sure to find staggeringly high rates of rape and domestic violence.

The problem with statistics is not that they aren't always reliable. That can be true, although in this case the numbers are likely conservative, since sexual violence is notoriously underreported. The problem with statistics is that they are easy to ignore. There is anonymity in numbers, which can make it hard to hold on to the facts—the people—behind them. Statistics are by definition impersonal. In order to make the problem of violence against women palpable we need to know the stories behind the numbers, which is why Africa captured my attention. Through Nolen and Lewis I saw the human faces behind the statistics, and they were ravaged yet resilient. The ravaging was almost beyond comprehension, but the resiliency was just as hard to grasp. It has taken me so long to work through the trauma of my rape and I have had all the benefits of a privileged upbringing in an affluent society with the full support of my family and community, the money to pay for counseling, the time to devote to it, and the law and criminal justice system on my side. How were these women and children, with more obstacles and fewer resources, managing?

Of all the stories in the news today, what is happening in the Democratic Republic of the Congo is the most disturbing. The country has been in the midst of a brutal civil war since the mid-90s and, from all accounts, the war within the war is a war on women's bodies. Sexual violence is being used as a weapon of war, and women are being subjected to brutal types of rape, sexual torture and mutilation. It is said that in parts of the eastern Congo it is more dangerous to be a woman than it is to be a soldier. Men are raping women in ways that are meant to maximize their humiliation and bring an end to any resistance. Women are raped in the presence of their husbands and gang-raped in front of crowds; sons are being forced to rape their mothers; and fathers are being forced to rape their daughters. And the nature of the raping is extremely violent. According to news reports women are first raped, and then often their vaginas are mutilated by knives, butchered by bayonets, or blown apart by guns. Let me say that again: women's vaginas are being mutilated by knives, butchered by bayonets, and blown apart by guns. The immediate goal here is no less than the complete destruction of the psychological and physical well being of women, with the broader aim of the obliteration of the social fabric of families and whole communities. It is a catastrophe. It is hard to believe that this is happening in the twenty-first century.

In the eastern Congolese town of Bukavu stands the Panzi General Hospital. Once a maternity hospital, it is now exclusively devoted to repairing women's vaginas. Dr. Denis Mukwege, a gynecologist and founder of the hospital, calls this war on women's bodies "sexual terrorism," since in his view words like "rape" and "sexual violence" fail to capture the utter devastation wreaked on these women's bodies. For over a decade, Dr. Mukwege and his fellow doctors have been surgically repairing and reconstructing the bodies of women whose genitals have been disfigured by sexual terrorism. The Panzi Hospital treats something like 3,500 rape victims a year, which may sound like a lot, but it is estimated that over 300,000 women and girls have suffered sexual violence during the civil war.

UN officials have called the eastern Congo the "rape capital of the world." The story of this war on women's bodies has received worldwide media coverage; it has been on the front page of the *New York Times*, and *60 Minutes* did a piece on it. The situation has also received support from some high-profile activists, including Eve Ensler, the award-winning American playwright and author of *The Vagina Monologues* and founder of V-Day, a global movement to stop violence against women and girls. Ensler has been doggedly lobbying for women's rights in the Congo for the last number of years, and V-Day, together with UNICEF, has begun a global campaign called Stop Raping our Greatest Resource: Power to Women and Girls of Democratic Republic of Congo. Stephen Lewis, who along with his other credits is now also one of the leading defenders of women's human rights, has designated sexual violence as one of the five areas of focus of the Stephen Lewis Foundation, a charity that supports community-based organizations in the fight against HIV/AIDS in Africa. Since its inception in 2003, the foundation has supported close to three hundred grassroots projects in fifteen sub-Saharan African countries, and in 2007 it began funding the Panzi Hospital and other initiatives in the Congo. Ever the humanitarian, Lewis tours the world with an urgent and impassioned plea for action. And he refuses to play politics; he has been sharply critical of the UN and of his own government's response to the crisis in the Congo.

According to recent reports, the Democratic Republic of the Congo is finally seeing some changes—tentative, but encouraging. The culture of impunity that rapists have long taken for granted is shifting thanks to increased pressure by certain international organizations working with the Congolese government. Aid agencies are helping to build courthouses and prisons across the eastern Congo, so that there is a place to put violent offenders. And Ensler, who has called the sexual terrorism in the

Congo a form of "femicide"—a systematic campaign to destroy women—is helping to build a safe place in Bukavu for rape survivors. It is taking the shape of a transitional housing complex and leadership center that is being called the City of Joy and will provide housing and counseling as well as leadership skills and self-defense training for survivors.

But perhaps the most positive change happening in the Congo is that women are speaking out against sexual violence. This is a culture where being raped brings shame not only to the woman or girl but also to her entire family, sometimes permanently. Yet in spite of the risk of being ostracized by their families and communities, despite the social stigma and fear of reprisal, women are vocalizing their opposition to rape. Local groups and activists are banding together, and with the support of organizations like V-Day and UNICEF, survivors are breaking the silence and telling their stories of rape.

By refusing to stay silent these survivors are helping to wage a counterattack in the war against women. As I discovered, talking about our experiences of sexual violence can be an important step in the recovery process for survivors—although not, perhaps, a necessary one. Anthropologists have been careful to note cross-cultural variation in the ways that women process and express their experiences of trauma, and, significantly, not all of them are verbal. Over time and across cultures women have relied on creative ways of communicating their experiences, which for some remain truly unspeakable. And while we usually narrate our experiences through language, we can also communicate through our actions and the choices we make in our lives each day. Testimony does not have to be spoken to be effective; there are other ways to express and show our hurt, other ways to protest.

Just because a woman does not put into words her experience of sexual violence does not mean that she has buried the truth of it. Still, as I learned, coming out as a rape survivor can go a long way toward erasing the humiliation that comes with having your body used sexually, violently, against your will. It is a way of telling the rest of the world that you have nothing to be ashamed of, which is just what these outspoken women in the Congo are doing, and, in the process, they are helping to draw international attention and aid to the crisis there. But the international community is not doing nearly enough. According to recent news reports and to the utter dismay of everyone working to end sexual violence in the country, despite small gains, the massacre of women continues.

*

In the winter leading up to my sabbatical I began to think seriously about writing this book, which is when I resolved to go to the Democratic Republic of the Congo and see firsthand the aftermath of sexual terrorism. I felt that I needed to come to grips with this war on women's bodies. There was a lacuna in my understanding of human nature. How could it be that women and children were being subjected to such extreme forms of sexual violence, and how was it possible that they found the will to survive? I wanted to go to Bukavu and visit Panzi Hospital. I wanted a chance to meet some of these brave women, but I was also hoping that I could help in some way. I had no money to give but I had some time. I thought that perhaps I could do volunteer work there during part of my sabbatical. At the time, I had read in a newspaper article that there was only one trauma counselor at the hospital—one single counselor! Though not a trained therapist, by 2008 I had been in therapy for long enough to know at least something about the therapeutic process. Over the years, I had also become interested in the concept of psychological trauma. I was fascinated by its history and by contemporary research into traumatic stress, which was advancing in multiple fields at a breakneck pace. I had started to do research in these areas back in 2001, just after I finished my PhD and before I started my job at the University of Guelph. By that point I had been in therapy with Anique for a couple of years and I had reached a stage in my recovery where I was feeling somewhat less fettered. This opened up some room for me to begin thinking philosophically about issues that, until then, I had been dealing with on a strictly personal level.

What I discovered back in 2001 was that I was in a good position to test my theoretical understanding against my personal experience, and I began to write about sexual violence and psychological trauma from a philosophical point of view. The writing was not easy, because it meant that I was always thinking about violence, rape, and trauma. Although I was not then writing about my own experience as a rape survivor this work was nevertheless quite triggering, bringing me back to memories and images that still overwhelmed me. It soon became clear that I was not yet free enough from the hold of my own experience to immerse myself in the research and writing full time. I continued to do research in the area over the next few years, but I also took long breaks from it.

It was around this same time, in the summer of 2002, that I began to come out as a rape survivor to friends and acquaintances. Although telling my story relieved me of a terrible burden, it was also stressful, adding to what was already shaping up to be a stressful year. I had just started my new job at the University of Guelph, and there were all the standard pressures that go along with that. As a backdrop, the relationship that I had been in since 1999, which had set me on the path to therapy and recovery, was beginning to break up. And, unfathomably, my brother-in-law, a new father to beautiful twins, was dying of brain cancer (a tragedy which had been my impetus to quit smoking earlier that year). PTSD is first and foremost a stress disorder, and although I was feeling less hemmed in by anxiety and panic than I had been a couple of years before, the stress of these events was too much for me.

To make matters worse, after having lived in Toronto since the fall of 1996, I uprooted myself and moved to Guelph, about an hour's drive from Toronto. At the time I weighed the strain of the commute against the stress of living alone in a new city, and I figured that the commute would be worse, so I rented a studio apartment on one of the main streets near the city's downtown. I spent that first year of my new job trying to cope with the various taxing events in my life while battling the anxiety that came from being on my own in an unfamiliar place. (In the end, I was wrong about the commute and I moved back to Toronto at the conclusion of that academic year.)

Guelph is a small, charming city with a population of about 120,000, but with an impressive amount of arts and culture for its size. It's got great music festivals and good bookstores and is consistently rated one of the country's best places to live, with low crime rates and a high standard of living. It is set in a pretty part of southwestern Ontario and has some gorgeous nineteenth-century limestone buildings dotted throughout the leafy downtown residential core, which is where my apartment was. I had a corner unit on the main floor of a three-storey walk-up, a few steps up from the street, with big windows facing an intersection on one side and a back lane on the other. The first thing I did when I moved in was buy security bars for my windows, but before installing them I decided to clear it by my landlord. I was worried that he might object to screw holes in the freshly painted window frames. I told him my plan and he looked at me like I was nuts. Security bars? Honestly? This was Guelph, he said, there was nothing to worry about here.

I was mortified and confused. Was I not at risk? I certainly felt unsafe, but was I really? Or was this yet another case of my wayward emotions overtaking reason? I wasn't sure what to think. I was already familiar enough with the statistics on sexual violence against women to know both that the problem was universal, which meant that sexual violence occurred all around the world, including in small, picturesque cities in Canada, and also that stranger rape was far less common than rape by a family member or intimate partner. So did I need bars on my windows or not? I resisted putting them up for a while out of embarrassment, but after one too many fitful sleeps I broke down and installed them on the windows that faced the back lane. At least this, I thought, I could justify. Still, it took me months to get comfortable enough in this new space to be able to get a sound night's sleep. The restless nights on top of the pressures of a new job, the tragedy of my brother-in-law's death, and the volatility of a relationship on its last legs was all too much for me and it triggered a relapse of sorts. The flashbacks and other intrusive thoughts became a daily affair once again. I was really struggling.

I drove into Toronto for my weekly appointments with Anique, but because I was going through a rough patch I thought I might also try something new, and so I ended up attending a few group therapy sessions for survivors of adult sexual assault. Up until that point I had been working on my recovery exclusively in a one-on-one context. I had read a handful of memoirs written by survivors of sexual violence, but I had never had the experience of being in a room with other rape survivors and exchanging stories. I went to these group sessions hoping that the solidarity I would find there would give me a new kind of understanding and, if I was lucky, further release from the grip of some of my more abiding symptoms.

I learned at least three important lessons from these sessions. The first was that women's experiences of rape rarely have the clear boundaries that mine had. Outside of war zones like the Congo, rape is not always or even usually life threatening, and it is not mainly perpetrated by strangers. At some level I already knew this. It is what all the data on rape says. And it is what I told myself as I struggled over the decision to install security bars in my apartment windows. Still, over the years, whenever I heard the word "rape" I imagined my hour of terror on boulevard Massena. And other first person accounts that I was familiar with—Alice Sebold's, Susan Brison's, Patricia Weaver Francisco's—were all cases of stranger rape and were all equally graphic. Without intending to, I had begun to identify rape with a series of actions that are not necessary or even typical characteristics of the crime. This is a conceptual mistake, one we are all at risk of making, goaded by the portrayal of sexual violence in the news and entertainment industries. And while my story is yet another extreme case of stranger rape, domestic violence, acquaintance and date rape, and childhood sexual abuse are by far the most pervasive forms of sexual violence worldwide. Amnesty International reports that most women know their abusers, who are most likely to be members of their own families. In Canada, for example, studies show that in cases reported to police, 80 percent of women know their attacker, and just about the same percentage of attacks happen in the home.

I went into these group sessions expecting to meet women whose stories closely resembled mine and I was genuinely surprised by what I heard instead. As it turned out, no one had a story quite like mine, which made me think that what Anique often said to me was true: people who go through what I went through do not typically live to talk about it. For the most part, these other women had been raped by men they knew—by husbands and ex-husbands, by boyfriends, by acquaintances, by men they had been out with on a date; in some cases they had been raped after trying to stop what had started out as a consensual romantic encounter—they had been raped after saying "no"; and many of them had been raped in their own homes or in dorm rooms on university campuses. These experiences were different enough from mine that for a moment I felt at risk of not finding the solidarity that I had come looking for, but it soon became clear that while the details of our experiences varied, each one of these women had had her body used—just like mine had been—sexually and against her will.

How to best define the concept of rape is a matter of some disagreement among philosophers. Is rape best understood as nonconsensual sex or forced sex—or both? Or maybe it is best defined as the threat of forced sex, which gets around cases where women have been rendered passive from drugs and are therefore not technically "forced." And does the state of mind of the rapist matter? Is it rape only if the rapist intends to rape, which might rule out cases where the rapist is extremely intoxicated or suffers a mental disability, rendering moot the issue of intent? And must the rapist reasonably believe that the woman has not consented?

These questions are pressing—how we define rape has important legal implications. And though I am not exactly sure how to best answer them, sitting through these group sessions showed me what rape is for rape survivors: it is the experience of being objectified, of having your body used forcibly, sexually, and violently. From this perspective, the state of mind of the rapist is pretty much irrelevant. For the rape survivor, sexual violence is a transgression of her personal autonomy and a violation of her bodily integrity. This is not to say that all women experience rape in the same way; they do not. In the first place, it depends on who the rapist is. If it is a stranger, well, that is one thing, but what if it is a father or an uncle or a teacher? When the violator is an authority figure, someone we are meant to trust, the shame and confusion that are part of the aftermath of sexual violence are intractably compounded.

What's more, a woman's experience of sexual violence is filtered through her understanding of the world and her place in it. Social, cultural, religious, and political circumstances all factor into the subjective quality of the experience of being raped. The right to personal autonomy may be universal in principle, for example, but I have to know that I have certain rights in order to feel wronged when those rights are breached. In a culture that does not recognize the autonomy of women, for example, where women do not have the right to make decisions for themselves, women might not experience sexual violence as a violation of their autonomy, even if they feel degraded and coerced.

Despite the differences in our stories, each one of the women who I met at these group sessions was shaken, each one battling with the consequences of sexual violence—the shame, the confusion, the onslaught of PTSD-related symptoms, and the estrangement from her own body, from her own sexuality. Each one had her own version of my hour of terror. In the end, it was easy to see myself in them.

The second lesson that I learned from these group sessions, which was reinforced each time I told my story anew to a friend, was that talking about what had happened to me helped me to feel whole. It allowed me to take this otherwise abstract and detached notion of myself as a "rape survivor" and integrate it into my self-image. Unlike combat fighting in war, rape is the kind of traumatic experience that individuals typically endure in isolation, and this can be difficult on a number of levels. There is something powerful about making public this private experience, about having others see us in it, about asking them to bear witness to our stories. This can help us fuse together the disparate parts of our identities, but also, in representing ourselves without disguise we allow others to see us for who we really are, giving them the chance to reflect our experiences back to us and, in doing so, treat us with dignity, and justice. Justice, understood in the broadest sense of being treated fairly by both individuals and social institutions, requires that our experiences in life be understood and properly reflected back to us.

Finally, these sessions gave me a glimpse into something important about the connection between theory and practice. I was the only survivor in the room who had done research in the area of trauma theory, and my participation reflected this dual point of view. Soon enough, over the course of a couple of meetings, the other women in the room began to turn to me with their questions. As a person who had some theoretical knowledge of psychological trauma and its aftermath and who had also lived through it, I came to be seen as something of an expert on the subject. Although I was not a trained therapist, this combination of theoretical understanding and lived experience seemed to offer a valuable perspective when it came to talking to other survivors. One thing I learned from this is that there are some phenomena, some experiences in life, which one has to live through to fully grasp.

I had this fact in mind in the time leading up to my sabbatical, which is why I thought I might be of some use at the Panzi Hospital as a trauma support counselor or facilitator. But I had no idea how to get there, or how to connect with the right sort of people who could help me get set up. Obviously I could not just show up in the eastern Congo with a sign saying "volunteer." I started by contacting some individuals at the Stephen Lewis Foundation, but I wasn't getting anywhere. And then I got lucky.

In the middle of the winter of 2008 an e-mail was sent to all faculty and staff at the University of Guelph announcing that the university was participating for the second consecutive year in a program called Leave for Change, a short-term volunteer placement initiative run by a Canadian program of international volunteer cooperation called Uniterra (jointly established by the Center for International Studies and Cooperation and the World University Service of Canada). The University of Guelph was the first university in Canada to participate in this program and, since 2007, in partnership with Uniterra, it has sponsored up to seven employees annually. Uniterra places volunteers in developing countries with the goal of reducing poverty and inequality around the world through what they call "capacity-building," where volunteers impart skills and knowledge that can outlive their short placements. Part of Uniterra's mandate is to promote the UN's millennium development goals, which include the promotion of gender equality and empowerment of women. I applied for a position, highlighting my knowledge of gender-based violence and my research and publications on the subject, and I also talked about my personal experience as a rape survivor, hoping that the combination would make me a suitable candidate. It worked. In April I learned that I had been accepted into the program. Uniterra sends volunteers to thirteen developing countries, including three in Africa, and I was slated to go to Maun, Botswana, in September of 2008, to work in a human rights organization called Women Against Rape (WAR). I could not believe my good fortune. With the support of the University of Guelph I would be traveling to sub-Saharan Africa to work at an organization whose mandate was the eradication of gender-based violence, and Uniterra would help to coordinate my travel and lodging and provide me with a network of support once I arrived. This was more than I could have ever hoped for. It felt like a once in a lifetime opportunity. The only problem was that I actually had to go to Africa. Alone.

*

In the decade following the rape, stuck in a pattern of reenactment and a series of bad choices, I took a handful of trips on my own, and each time I found myself in an unending state of hyperarousal. There were those first trips to Paris and New York, and then Europe a few years after that, followed by another cross-country solo driving trip, and a few brief excursions to the United States to visit friends. Over the years I had become so accustomed to the anxiety and panic that was with me wherever I traveled that I had normalized it. But it had gotten so bad that just getting on a plane was a hurdle to overcome, and I could not do so without being properly medicated. I would take a clonazepam or two and then top that off with a couple of drinks. It was only after I started work in therapy that I realized how taxing it had been on me to travel on my own, and I was a bit concerned about how my body would react to being alone halfway around the world in Botswana. Uniterra had an

impressive framework of support set up for volunteers
in partnering countries, and I knew that I would be well
taken care of while I was away, but as I said before, the
way my body responds to traumatic triggers does not
necessarily track my beliefs about my personal safety.

Sure enough, in the months leading up to my departure I noticed my breathing beginning to shorten, and
so I scheduled a couple of extra therapy sessions with
Anique. I was beyond excited to be going to Botswana,
but I hadn't even gotten on the plane and my body was
already reacting to the stress of being on my own in an
unfamiliar place. I wondered how I was going to manage once I arrived, but over the years I have developed a
number of ways to coax my body out of thinking it is in
danger in order to bring it down from a state of hyperarousal. I lay on Anique's couch and rehearsed responses
to familiar triggers, strategies for trying to stay grounded.
In the weeks before leaving I tried to keep focused on the
excitement of the adventure I was about to embark on,
persuading my body not to misinterpret the adrenaline
of excitement for that brought on by fear. I left Toronto
feeling as well prepared as I could be, and with a huge
stash of clonazepam as backup.

I had done some reading on Botswana before I left
and I had a rough understanding of the history, politics,
and economics of the country. Botswana is located in
southern Africa, landlocked between South Africa, Na-
mibia, Zimbabwe, and Zambia. It is, by all accounts, an
African success story. Formerly a British protectorate,
Botswana gained independence in 1966, and since then
the country has had one democratically elected leader
after another, making it the continent's longest continu-

ous multiparty democracy. Politically stable, it was one of the poorest countries in Africa when it gained independence, but shortly thereafter it was discovered that it was rich in diamonds. It is now the largest diamond exporter in Africa. It is also rich in cattle, which is its second largest export after diamonds and, at least historically, a determinant of a family's social status—more cattle, higher status (I have heard Botswana called a "cattle-ocracy"). Botswana has one of the fastest growth rates in per capita income since independence, and during the last forty years it graduated from a so-called low-income country to a middle-income country. It boasts good infrastructure development, and its impressive network of roads helps to move people and goods across the country (this is a double-edged victory: easy mobility is often cited as a contributing factor to the spread of HIV/AIDS, because it facilitates multipartner sexual activity among migrant workers).

Botswana also has a thriving tourist trade. It is a stunning country, rich in wildlife and remarkably well preserved. The land is flat with gentle undulations, and some 85 percent of it is covered by the Kalahari Desert. The unspoiled Okavango Delta, the largest inland delta in the world, can be found in the northwest. It is fed from the north by the Okavango River, which drains inland from Angola. It is a mix of dryland and wetland, making for some of the best wildlife viewing in all of Africa. To create a sustainable tourism industry the country abandoned mass tourism and adopted instead what it calls "high quality/low volume" tourism. Its high-end photographic safaris in the delta are some of the top rated in Africa and draw tourists from all over the world.

Botswana's hard-earned reputation as an African success story has taken a hit in the last ten years, with the HIV/AIDS crisis. The first case of HIV/AIDS in Botswana was diagnosed in 1985, and it now has the second-highest prevalence rate in the world, with an estimated 350,000 people living with the disease. Botswana is a sparsely populated country, with 1.7 million people, which means that the prevalence rate is hovering around 23 percent. Among its adult population, the rate is closer to 37.3 percent; approximately 1 out of every 3 adults is living with the disease. Life expectancy at birth has dropped dramatically over the last decade, from 68 years to 39. Half of the pregnant women aged 30–34 years who were tested at prenatal clinics in 2005 were infected with HIV, and the rate was just slightly lower (45 percent) for women aged 25–29 years. Botswana's young adult population is sick and dying off, and 95,000 children have lost at least one parent to HIV/AIDS. The situation has had an irrevocable economic and social cost. It is nothing short of apocalyptic.

The government declared the epidemic a national emergency and instituted a progressive nationwide program for dealing with the disease, including free testing and free antiretroviral drugs for all citizens. This is the first program of its kind in Africa, and the world is watching to see if it works. There is also a decade-old public awareness campaign, seen on billboards across the country, advertising the ABCs of sex: abstain, be faithful, and condomize. To be successful these initiatives need to do more than just decrease the spread of the disease. HIV/AIDS in Africa is not just a medical problem; it is a social and economic problem. In Botswana the economy is

facing the loss of a significant portion of its adult work-
force, and aside from the short-term direct impact that
this has on businesses (from absentee workers to high
labor turnover), the long-term costs are hard to quantify.

The social impact of HIV/AIDS in Botswana exposes
some of the structural inequalities embedded in the culture. In Botswana, as in many countries in Africa that
have been hard-hit by HIV/AIDS, the ways that families
are living together has changed. As parents of young children succumb to the disease the responsibility of caring
for the children falls to the extended family, disproportionately to the elderly women. Grandmothers are in the
horrible position of having to bury their own children
and then immediately move on from that painful loss in
order to take care of their orphaned grandchildren, often
with few extra resources to do so.

In Botswana, HIV/AIDS is most commonly transmit-
ted through heterosexual sex, where unequal power relations between men and women characterize relationships. Women have fewer legal rights than men, and
social and cultural practices reinforce long-standing gender inequalities. Traditionally, Botswana women and children were considered the property of men, either their
fathers or husbands. This was almost universally true
prior to the nineteenth century, when rape was viewed
as a crime against the male parent, whose virgin daughter
was spoiled (a crime which could be repaid by the rapist
marrying the sullied woman, either willingly or by coer-
cion), but traces of this way of thinking are still strong and
enforced legally.

Botswana's legal system includes both common law
and customary law. While common law is codified, cus-

tomary laws are unique to particular tribes or communities; the laws are not documented but are passed on
orally through community leaders. With respect to common law, there have been a number of recent changes
that have improved the lot of women within the family.
Most significantly, the Abolition of Marital Powers Act
of 2005 gives both partners in common law marriage
equal powers within the family, whereas married women
were previously regarded as minors, and thus needed the
consent from their husband, for instance, to carry out a
financial transaction.

However, in contrast to common law, customary law
and practice continue to perpetuate structural inequalities between men and women, which is particularly
problematic since 80 percent of legal cases are heard in
customary courts (there are over five hundred of these
spread across the country). For example, women who
are married under customary law are not covered by
the legislation on the abolition of marital power. Men
continue to be regarded as the head of the family, with
guardianship rights over women and children. Marital
rape is not illegal under customary law. It is commonly
believed that men have certain conjugal rights within a
marriage, a notion that is widespread, extending beyond
the borders of Botswana and also dating back to the eigh-
teenth century, to the idea that a wife consents to sexual
intercourse in perpetuity by signing a marital contract,
at which time she essentially becomes the property of
her husband. Marital immunity for rape is still common
today in dozens of countries around the world, and in
many of those where wife rape is illegal it remains widely
tolerated and is seen as a husband's prerogative. (In the

United States, for instance, criminal codes in all fifty states had marital rape exemption laws until 1976, which meant that husbands could not be prosecuted for raping their wives; all states have had laws against marital rape since the mid-1990s, but in the majority of them there are exemptions from rape prosecution given to husbands, an indication that rape within marriage is still regarded as a lesser offense than other kinds of rape.)

What's more, in Botswana a mother has no maintenance rights when a child is born out of wedlock, and the father has no duty to support the child, although he is supposed to pay the mother's father for damaging her reputation (yet another instance of the idea that rape is a wrong committed against the male head of the family because he is the one who suffers through the loss of the value of the woman). Inheritance rights are also inequitable. If there is no written will, which is usually the case, then the female children's rights are trumped by their brothers'.

While the law does not dictate morality it is often a reflection of it. The structural inequalities that favor men over women and are supported in customary law and practice are rooted in cultural stereotypes. In matters of family and relationships, women and girls in Botswana have considerably fewer rights than men and boys. This is why the spread of HIV/AIDS reflects a kind of gender injustice. Women and girls lack the authority to negotiate appropriate sexual relations, which contributes to the pervasiveness of intimate partner assault, rape, and other forms of sexual violence, which in turn makes women and girls more susceptible to the spread of HIV. The material advantage that older men have over younger girls

furthers the power imbalance by making young girls re-
liant on men for financial stability, in turn making them
vulnerable to intergenerational sexual violence. Incest is
also a serious problem, in particular the rape of young
girls by their stepfathers, with orphaned children being
the most vulnerable group. It is no surprise that women
and girls make up the fastest growing demographic of
HIV/AIDS in the country.

And just like we have seen in so many parts of the
world, speaking out about rape or incest here is an act
that is seriously frowned on and can result in potentially
devastating, even fatal consequences for survivors. Children are taught not to talk about "family secrets," and
survivors wind up burying their experiences out of ne-
cessity. But, as I learned from my own experience, there
can be a steep psychological price to this, and in this case
it is a cost endured not only by single individuals and
families, but by a whole country.

*

WAR is a nongovernmental organization located in
Maun, a town of about fifty thousand people located
in the Ngamiland district in northwestern Botswana, at
the southernmost tip of the Okavango Delta. WAR was
founded in 1993 by a group of women who came together
following the nonprosecution of white farmers after
the rape of three Basarwa women (Basarwa, otherwise
known as San or Bushmen, are an indigenous people
of Botswana). WAR's mandate is to support abused
women and children and address the underlying issues
of gender inequity that contribute to their abuse. In the
fall of 2008, during my brief visit, there were about a

dozen staff members, a couple of local volunteers, and a long-term volunteer from the Peace Corps. WAR is Botswana's only rape crisis center. It offers counseling to survivors and their families; it has an education department, which works closely with some of the schools in the area; and it has an advocacy department, whose members travel around the district bringing awareness of gender-based violence to rural communities.

I flew from Toronto via Frankfurt to Johannesburg, and from there I took a plane to Gaborone, Botswana's capital city, where I had an orientation before flying to Maun the next day. When I arrived in Gaborone I was jet-lagged and my breathing was constricted, but I was thrilled to be there. I was awestruck by the sultry beauty of the place. I was expecting Botswana to be stunning, but nothing prepared me for the intoxicating smell of the sun on the sand, which hit me the moment I stepped outside of the airport. If you can imagine the crackling, wonderfully peaty smell of burning leaves, and then substitute sun-bleached white, hot Kalahari sand for the leaves, you are close. It is impossible not to be impressed by the grace of the land.

I was in Botswana for three weeks, but with a few days in Gaborone bookending my time in Maun, I was at WAR for just over two weeks. The senior staff had written out a job description for me, which I had received before I left, so I had some sense of their expectations. They wanted me to meet with staff members to trade information about gender-based violence, and hopefully bring an international perspective to the issues, but they were particularly keen about the fact that I was a rape survivor who was out of the closet. Though it is hard to quantify, it is clear that there is value in being outspoken as a rape survivor in a culture where social taboos strictly limit the solidarity that women who have suffered sexual violence are able to find from each other. The staff at WAR wanted me to meet with other rape survivors and talk to them about my personal experience; they were also hoping that I could serve as a case in point about the universality of sexual violence. I was hoping that in just two short weeks I would be able to have some kind of impact.

The staff at WAR arranged for me to stay in a one-bedroom apartment in a single-story gated apartment complex with twenty-four-hour security, which is a fairly common form of urban dwelling in Botswana, especially for foreigners, although mine was the only one of its kind on a sandy road that was otherwise sprinkled with traditional round thatched huts. It was located about a ten-minute drive from the downtown, where the WAR office was situated, just down the street from the local airport. I arrived in sunny Maun in the late morning, eager with anticipation and already exhilarated by the adventure. With an irrepressible smile I met the staff at WAR and then spent the better part of the afternoon getting settled into my temporary home before starting work the next day. There is no easy public transportation in Maun, and in any case taxis are the best way to get around as a tourist, and also the safest for a woman traveling on her own, and so the staff at WAR had hooked me up with one of their favorite taxi drivers. He took me to and from work every day and carted me around Maun whenever I needed to get somewhere. On that first day he dropped me off in town so that I could do some grocery shopping and get some household supplies for the next couple of weeks, and then he returned me back to my apartment later in the day.

The apartment was sparsely furnished with a chair, a couch, a bed, a dresser, a TV, and plenty of bugs, which came out mostly at night and justified the mosquito net I had draped from the overhead light above the bed. But the space was perfectly comfortable, and on my first afternoon there I unpacked my clothes and put away my groceries while listening to the nearby laughter of some neighborhood kids. It is true that I was having some anxiety, but it was nothing that I couldn't handle. Besides, I was almost too excited to notice it. I could barely believe that here I was, in Africa. I had traveled by myself across hemispheres and I had made it—so far, so good. I had bought some food for dinner at a take-out restaurant in town, and I tucked into that while flipping channels between a couple of local television stations. I popped a clonazepam and went to bed early, eager for what was coming next.

*

My first full day of work started early, at 8 a.m., and the first half hour of that day set the tone for the next two weeks. Every morning the staff at WAR gather in the main office for a meeting to kick off the day. The proceedings are easygoing and upbeat. Senior staff members deliver updates on their latest activities, announcements are made, and anybody who has something to say says it. I observed all of this with great interest, doing my best to follow along, and then the most unexpected thing happened. The entire staff broke into a song, a rousing and mellifluous hymn with African melodies and irrepressible joy. I was floored. When the song ended someone said a prayer and, with delicate charm, the workday began.

I spent two weeks intoxicated by the power of these songs. The extraordinary people who work at WAR face the harsh facts of sexual violence on a daily basis, and they are devoted to helping survivors soften the edges of its bleak repercussions. Frontline workers all over the world face similar challenges, but at least in some parts of the world you can count on institutional backing from relevant stakeholders. In Botswana there is some high-level political will calling for an end to gender-based violence, but the structural inequalities that we see reflected in customary law are so thoroughly lodged in the culture that institutional support lags behind. Perpetrators of violence often get off with impunity, and the support that WAR gets from the local authorities is inconsistent at best. Moreover, like many similar kinds of organizations, WAR is underfunded and overburdened. Others might crumple under the weight of it all, yet the staff here remains ebullient. Day after day, they belt out these harmonious tunes, and then get on with the business of helping people heal from the trauma of sexual violence. It is an inspiring display of generosity of spirit.

On the Friday that ended my second week, the counselors organized a group session for individuals in the community who were survivors of sexual violence. They wanted me to lead the discussion portion of the session and tell the story of my rape, highlighting both key aspects of my recovery as well as ongoing challenges. I had spent most of the previous two weeks talking with the these counselors, exchanging personal and professional knowledge about gender-based violence and psycho-

logical trauma, and I had also written a few reports to
serve as the basis for some upcoming conference presen-
tations that various staff members were planning to give.
This had all felt like useful, good work, and like I was ful-
filling Uniterra's mandate of "capacity building," though
in truth I was learning as much from the staff at WAR as
they could have possibly been learning from me. But the
group session gave me a chance to have a real impact,
and I was grateful for the opportunity to be a part of it.

The session was led by the senior counselor at WAR,
with the help of a junior counselor, and besides me there
were seven participants, including two young girls, aged
six and nine, two teenagers, two young women in their
twenties, and a woman in her fifties. The fact that there
were these young girls in the group was hard to stomach—a blunt reminder that sexual violence does not dis-
criminate by age. This session was the most effectively
run group session that I had ever attended. It was filled
with activities that were meant to emphasize the impor-
tance of community and the role of others in the healing
process. At one point, using simple props, the counselors
demonstrated our inability to complete a basic task on
our own, a tangible illustration of our dependence on
others for recovery. We started the session by standing
up and singing, swaying our hips, clapping and laugh-
ing. It was just the kind of ice-breaker that you hope for
to help ease the difficulty of the discussion that's coming
next. The two youngest girls, whose teacher had come
with them, sang and danced with us but did not participate in the discussion. Instead, they sat in a corner,
playfully drawing while the rest of us gathered in a circle
to talk.

I started the discussion by telling the story of my rape. I spoke in English, which is the official language of Botswana and is widely spoken throughout the developed areas of the country, but I paused after each sentence so that one of the counselors could translate each sentence into Tswana, the national language of Botswana. I talked in detail about what had happened to me, and then I talked in general terms about psychological trauma and recovery. When I was done there were a few moments of silence, and I wondered what was going through the minds of the other participants. Had I broken some cultural norm in telling my story in all its graphic precision? Had I offended them? Or had I spoken too generally, not gone into enough detail? Or were they simply not interested? But I just needed to be patient. After some time, one by one, each woman raised her hand to speak, and before long they were peppering me with questions.

Did my rapist use a condom? Was I afraid to leave my house afterward? For how long? Did I tell my family what happened? Were they mad at me? How did it feel to go back to school after? Was I afraid to sleep at night? Did I drink and use drugs? Still? What about boyfriends? What about sex? One of the women in her twenties told me that she had no idea that people in countries like Canada were subject to rape. Another said that she had never heard anyone speak publicly about rape. And one of the teenagers told me in an indelible moment that hearing my story would change her future because it showed her that recovery is possible. We finished the session by drawing a picture of an imaginary garden, our own make-believe sanctuary. The young girls were welcomed back into the group to make garden drawings, and afterward we shared our pictures of our safe havens and our hopes for a nonviolent future.

*

I wished that I had had more time to spend in Maun. I had been lucky enough to go on a weekend safari in the Delta, where I experienced in all its glory the grace and allure of the African landscape. I also got to know some wonderful people in Maun, who welcomed me into their homes and looked after me with care, from my taxi driver, who might well have been the most cheerful guy in all of Botswana, to the academics and artists I met, who invited me to their dinner parties and introduced me to their friends. But beyond all that, in just a couple of quick weeks, I had made fast friends with the staff at WAR. I had developed a real affection for them, heightened by the intensity and intimacy of our time together, in particular for the counselors, with whom I spent most of my time, but for the rest of the staff as well, who all helped to create an impassioned workplace, and after such a short visit I was not quite ready to leave. I had learned a lot from watching these people in action, and I had been moved and inspired by the group session in ways that I could not have predicted. Certainly, I would have liked to have spent more time with the other women and girls who I met that day, maybe arranged for a second group session or been able to talk with some of them one-on-one. After I had told my story a few of them opened up about their own experiences with sexual violence, but our time that day was coming to an end and I was left yearning for the opportunity of another meeting.

We all milled about on that Friday afternoon after the group session broke up, counselors and participants alike, drinking juice and chatting about nothing much. The weather was blistering, as usual, but the fierce sun gave off a dry heat, and it was just another gorgeous day in Botswana. I was talking to the junior counselor when the teacher approached me to ask me how much longer I was going to be in Maun. She wanted me to come speak at her school in front of the whole assembly of students. She said that most of them would have never heard anyone speak publicly about sexual violence, and this could be an opportunity for them to have that experience. I felt honored by this request, and more than anything I wished that I could have stayed longer and been able to talk to these young kids, but I was leaving Maun early Monday morning, and so I never got the chance.

*

Not everyone who lives through a potentially traumatic event becomes psychologically traumatized. Some people who experience sudden acts of terror and violence recover relatively easily, while others face a lifelong battle. Again, expert opinion on the matter suggests that there are predisposing genetic and environmental factors that impact a person's resiliency to the experience of extreme stress. I grew up in a privileged environment with my basic material and physical needs all accounted for, but it is possible that my emotional neurocircuitry went awry at a young age, perhaps as a result of needing more attention from my parents than they were able to give or for some other environmental or genetic reason, which would have meant that I was prone to anxiety be-

fore I was raped. This might help to explain the intensity of my PTSD-related symptoms, but another aspect
that shapes a person's response to traumatic stress is the
severity of the traumatic experience. When these factors
conspire against an individual she is left psychologically
traumatized, and the emotional, cognitive, and physiological consequences can last a lifetime. This is true universally, even if the experience and aftermath of trauma
varies historically and culturally. For as long as we can
remember individuals who have survived acts of terror
have been incapacitated by the experience, which is not
to say that the symptoms of trauma are universal. While
there are likely a number of core features of trauma that
are constant across variables, trauma theorists argue
that the nuances of how these symptoms manifest vary
along social and historical norms.

Psychological trauma as a consequence of terrifying life events no doubt predates Erichsen's diagnosis
of railway spine as a nervous disorder. And as modern
neuroimaging techniques improve it is likely that we
will further confirm what a growing number of people
who work in the field already believe, which is that
psychological trauma is at least in part—and maybe in
large part—rooted in a biochemical reaction to extreme
stress.

But the history of PTSD is a story not of biology but
of social action, of the politics of diagnosis and disease.
PTSD, as we currently understand it, as characterized
by an environmental event and by a set of persistent
symptoms, is relatively new. As this recent history tells
us, PTSD made it into the *DSM* because a group of psychiatrists and veteran activists worked tenaciously for

years to get it in there. But the encyclopedic style and dry tone of the manual belies this history. *DSM* entries, like those in many scientific reference books, sound like descriptions of immutable matters of fact, which gives the impression that PTSD is a psychiatric illness which has been with us for all time, prevalent yet undetected, until its discovery in the 1970s. This is both true and false. It is true that throughout history people all over the world have endured debilitating emotional, cognitive, and physiological problems as a result of terrorizing life experiences. That is an objective matter of fact. It is a truth that is passed down orally in some cultures and in others recorded in history books and depicted in movies and novels. It is a fact that can be checked and verified. Those who suffer from psychological trauma may experience the immutability of its symptoms as I have.

But it is false that PTSD, at least as we currently understand it, was "out there," lying dormant, until veteran and feminist activists brought it to the surface. And this is importantly false, because how we categorize and label people influences how they see themselves. Categorizations are not given by the world. We make them up, and they can come bundled with moral significance—certain categories of people are good (volunteer workers), for instance, and certain categories are bad (pedophiles); there are certain categories of people who we try to help (orphans) and others who we try to control (rebellious teenagers).

The way we categorize people impacts how we interact with them, which in turn impacts how they view themselves. The way that we categorize a rock, on the other hand, doesn't impact the rock, which is strictly unaware of our opinion of it and is therefore not capable of being influenced by it. But people are not indifferent to the ways we categorize them, and this can have a serious impact on someone, especially when there is a value attached to the labeling. Being identified as a rape survivor, for instance, means that people view me in certain ways—as someone to be pitied, for instance. But knowing that others view me in this way makes me rebel against any tendency to self-pity; it makes me work hard to be less deserving of others' pity. This in turn makes people pity me less, which in turn and over time changes what it means to be a rape survivor.

Philosophers have characterized this process as a looping effect. As more rape survivors speak out about what has happened to them, as they gain strength through their own recovery, we might still feel compassion for them, but we might be less inclined to feel sorry for them. And as they become aware of that fact, they may be less inclined to feel sorry for themselves. Through this feedback loop we can change what it means to be a rape survivor, and this is why it is crucial to understand what's false about the idea that PTSD has been around forever. How we treat people shapes how they come to see themselves, and how people see themselves influences how they behave and thus who they become. As we learn more about the influence and impact of traumatic stress we change the ways that we interact with people with PTSD, and this changes those people. Some have suggested that it can even change their past.

I began to understand this idea of a looping effect in a tangible way years ago, when I was knee-deep into my work in therapy. Of all of my trauma-related problems, the thing that bothered me the most was my tendency to react irrationally to triggering situations. First as a philosophy student and then as a professional philosopher, I took great pride in my ability to think and reason analytically. And yet there were these moments in my life, like the night that I spent in the police station in Paris waiting for Robert to track me down and kill me, or sitting outside Café Le Conti drinking a mid-morning espresso, trying to calm down my racing heart, or driving around in my Honda Accord sure that someone was hiding in the hatch waiting to attack, where I was overcome by a fear that I could identify as unfounded, but which I could not reason myself out of. This pattern persisted over the years, and it was maddening. With each new instance—tiptoeing around my apartment in Toronto, peering out the peephole, searching for intruders—I would get increasingly upset with myself, unable to make sense of why I could not persuade myself out of these irrational responses. I could not understand why evidence held no sway over me—why my fear was impervious to it. This took a real toll on my self-esteem.

Years later, when I started to understand these features of my thoughts and behaviors as symptomatic of PTSD, I reevaluated this tendency of mine in a new light. Most importantly, I no longer saw myself as irrational, because I began to understand that the experience of feeling afraid—in my car, on a busy street, or in my apartment—was not a cognitive response to any present circumstance but rather a complex neurobiological one. These recalcitrant emotions—fear in the acknowledged absence of danger—can be resistant to evidence. They may be triggered by something in our external environment but they are calibrated to the trauma that is lodged in the body, and not to anything in the here and now. In each of these instances my body was reacting as if it were under threat, even though it patently wasn't. As I began to learn more about PTSD I realized that this kind of somatic response, riddled with anxiety and a constant expectation of catastrophe, was typical among those who have survived traumatic events. This gave new meaning to my past actions, and I began to feel more normal. My self-esteem got the break that it badly needed.

*

The way that people suffer from terrorizing life experiences has changed over time and along cultural lines. In the same way that a woman's experience of rape is filtered through her beliefs regarding her right to make decisions about her own body, our posttraumatic experience is lived through our social and cultural commitments. And because human beings are dynamic, we need to be careful about the assumptions we make regarding people's experiences, as those assumptions will bear on how we interact with them. This is particularly important for clinicians, therapists, and mental health workers to keep in mind. I did not want to assume the universality of PTSD as I was talking with other rape survivors in Botswana, and I was cautious about employing Western psychological concepts. I did not know what sorts of intricate social realities were embedded in their cultural framework, and I did not know how these realities would be reflected in their understanding of rape, trauma, and recovery.

And yet I could not help but see that these women were just like me: scared, vulnerable, and ashamed—and relieved to have a safe place where they did not have to hide their truth. Each survivor in that room had been treated as an object, each one had had her body used sexually, violently, against her will. We sat there in appreciation of the support that we were getting from each other. As I looked around the room I saw empathy in the faces of these other women. I found strength in the experience of hearing their stories, and I could see this fortitude mirrored in their expressions as they listened to mine. We nodded along in agreement while one woman talked about feeling estranged from her own body, her friends, even her family. We identified with another's anxiety about leaving her house once the sun went down. Another woman talked about her fear of running into her rapist, and we all held our breath in understanding. And when one woman talked about the humiliation of having her body defiled with utter indifference, we all quietly concurred.

These women knew precisely what I was talking about when I referred to my sleepless nights, my fast-beating heart, and my not-infrequent reliance on alcohol or drugs to get me through difficult times. The safety of the space created by the counselors gave us the opportunity to be honest about our experiences, and there was a palpable dignity in the room as we told our stories and had them reflected back to us. And this is why it is important to understand what's true about the idea that psychological trauma has been around forever. Because despite the differences in the ways that people experience sexual violence, there is something universal about rape and its aftermath. And so it was that the solidarity that I found in the group sessions that I had attended in Canada five years earlier was recreated halfway around the world in Maun, Botswana.

5: Paris, Revisited

In late August 2009, I returned to Paris for the first time in fifteen years. Although I had been back a number of times in the first few years following the rape, I had never revisited the scene of the crime. Now, close to twenty years later, I was ready to do so. I spent the summer anticipating the trip, not quite sure what to expect from it. I wondered how I would feel walking up to number 142 boulevard Massena. Would my body be stuck in a series of flashbacks? Would the apartment building look as I remembered it? Would I collapse upon seeing it? Although I was prepared to find out, I was relieved that I wouldn't have to go through this alone. I would be going on this journey with my partner, Bruce, who I began seeing in the spring of 2004 and with whom I am in it for the long haul. Bruce had an in-depth understanding of my stress disorder, and it was reassuring to know that he would be by my side as I traveled back to the night of August 1, 1990.

We had planned our trip around a work conference. We flew into Paris and took a shuttle train from Charles de Gaulle to Gare du Nord and then hopped a train to Amsterdam, where I was scheduled to give a talk. The idea was to go to Amsterdam first so that I could get work out of the way and have a few days to settle in and get over the jet lag before our excursion to Paris. I had not been to Amsterdam since 1990, and I had spent much of my time then in coffee shops, smoking pot. This time I got a real taste of the city, which is a mecca in Europe for arts and culture enthusiasts. Our hotel was located on one of the remarkable seventeenth-century canals that form a belt around the city, and when I wasn't busy at my conference Bruce and I would stroll around the canals, venturing out from the city center into some of Amsterdam's charming neighborhoods, stopping in at museums and marveling at the outstanding historical architecture. There is a relaxed allure to this city that makes it feel approachable, easily livable, and we had a great few days there, not thinking too much about Paris and what was coming next.

Then, in the early afternoon of Friday August 21, 2009, Bruce and I boarded a train at Amsterdam Central Station that was headed for Paris. I was retracing my steps, taking the same route that I had taken on August 1, nineteen years earlier. I had been feeling relatively at ease in Amsterdam. I had been enjoying myself and was not feeling too stressed in anticipation of returning to Paris, but that changed once we were on the train. I tried to get lost in the beauty of the countryside but I was starting to feel my breath riding on the surface. By the time we arrived in Paris my stress level had begun to peak, the laid-back atmosphere of our time in Amsterdam suddenly long gone. We took the Metro from Gare du Nord to the sixth arrondissement and got off at Saint-Germain-des Prés, the Metro stop just across the street from our hotel. We checked in and by chance landed a room on the top floor of the building. The room was small, but it was the only one in the hotel with an outdoor terrace overlooking the rooftops of Paris. The terrace was about the same size as the room, approximately 150 square feet, with a wrought-iron table and chairs, and it would have been a romantic place to hang out, drink wine, and eat cheese, if I hadn't been otherwise preoccupied.

We wandered around the city a bit that evening, but I wasn't much in the mood for sightseeing. The plan was to go to the apartment first thing the next morning, and I wanted to make it an early night. At times like this, when my body is verging on a state of hyperarousal, I tend to try to manage my stress by controlling my environment. That night what I needed was a quiet room and a lot of personal space. It's not that I wanted to be alone; I was happy to have Bruce with me, and in moments like this I am comforted by his mere presence, but I did not want him coming anywhere near me. I did not want physical contact of any sort—no hugs, no kisses, no closeness. I pushed him clear over to his side of the bed, only half-jokingly, and settled in for a restless night's sleep.

We woke up early on Saturday morning, had some coffee, got dressed, and off we went. We took the Metro and then a bus to boulevard Massena. The bus dropped us off just down the street from number 142. We crossed the wide boulevard and walked up to the apartment building, and then around to the side, just off the street, where the glass entranceway is located. I had been anticipating this moment for months, unable to imagine how I would simply walk my way through it, but I was surprised to find that my legs were holding up just fine. The glass doors that opened to the outside were unlocked and so we went into the lobby, where I snapped pictures and paced, stunned, showing Bruce where I broke free, and where the dentist and his companion were standing when I grabbed onto them. It was a surreal moment and I was doing my best to take it all in.

As I said earlier, my memory of the apartment building was a bit off. In my mind it was lush, whereas in fact the outside of the building was unremarkable and the inside, though not exactly dingy, was not exactly fancy, either, with concrete hallways and a bad paint job. But the lobby did have a kind of opulence to it, with marble floors and a giant glass chandelier reflecting off a large mirrored wall. I wanted to get inside the building, but the interior set of glass doors was locked, so we waited. After a while a resident showed up and fortunately didn't hesitate to let us follow him inside. We rode the elevator up to the tenth floor and we walked along the hallway, past the center block of lockers and around the corner to face apartment 1070. I stood there, legs still holding up, staring at the door, amazed to be back.

Eventually I decided to knock, and a slight woman who looked to be in her fifties opened up the door a crack, just enough for me to peer in, and I began to ramble in my broken French about something that had happened to me *"il y a vingt ans"*—twenty years ago. I probably sounded more than a bit crazy, and as I was asking her if we could come in she simply closed the door on us, which, I suppose, was just as well. I am not sure that I needed to see the inside of the apartment again. But back at the other end of the hallway, on the wall just opposite the elevator, we discovered a floor plan, a *plan d'evacuation*, which showed the interior layout of all the apartments on the tenth floor. Apartment 1070 was exactly as I had remembered it: the galley kitchen directly in front of the door, the narrow hallway extending to the right with two rooms off to the left, and a bathroom at the end of the hall. I found it reassuring that my memory of the apartment had not failed me, and, as proof, I took a bunch of pictures of the floor plan before riding the elevator down to the second floor to see if, by any chance, the dentist was still running his practice out of the building.

I was pretty sure I knew precisely which door was his, but the woman who answered the door and our query told us that we needed to go down one more floor. This initially confused me, because I was sure that on the night of August 1, 1990, we had climbed up only one flight of stairs from the lobby to the dentist's office, but then I remembered that in Paris (like in much of Europe) the main floor of most buildings is not "1" but "0." So the dentist, who apparently was still practicing in the building, did indeed have an apartment one floor above the lobby—on the first floor. We walked down a flight of stairs and found a door with his nameplate on it, across the hall from where I remembered it to be. We knocked and waited, and then knocked again, but there was no answer. I didn't know if his office doubled as his home residence, and we wondered if he wasn't there because it was a Saturday. I was disappointed. In the time that it had taken us to walk down one floor I had become excited to learn that, after all this time, the dentist was still around, and it would have been good to have been able to talk to him. The last time I had seen him, at the trial, I had been so broken. I would have liked to connect with him again, to have had the chance to tell him that I had come out the other side and that I was, now, more or less fine. I would have told him that I had started to write a book about my experience. For the rest of our time in Paris I toyed with the idea of going back to boulevard Massena to try his door once more, but I could not muster the energy. In the end, one visit had been enough.

I had taken a clonazepam earlier that morning to help steel myself for the outing, which had been easier than I had anticipated. I walked through the lobby and along the hallways and down the stairs of the apartment building feeling strong, feeling like I had won. I faced apartment 1070 directly and it did not break me. There were no flashbacks to endure and no demons to face, aside from my own reflection in the lobby mirror. This time I had come to France prepared, and I didn't need a bad falafel to give me an excuse to stay inside, as I had back in 1994. This time I had a certain awareness of how triggering the experience could be, and I had been able to process that in advance. Finally, the emotional hold that boulevard Massena had had over me for close to two decades had been deflated.

We took a bus and then the Metro back to the sixth arrondissement and bummed around for a while. We wandered into the fancy shops in and around rue Saint-Germain-des-Prés and I decided to buy myself a pair of expensive shoes, a reward for the morning's work. I was feeling pretty high—accomplished, even—at least for a few hours, but as the day wore on my frame of mind took a nosedive. I guess it would have been too much to expect my emotions to cruise unadulterated while I retraced my steps to 142 boulevard Massena, and I fell into a funk. I didn't develop a stomach flu, but I did spend the rest of the night in a foul mood. I picked fights with Bruce, rehearsing a familiar pattern, pushing him until he fought back, our words as knowing weapons against each other's weaknesses, and then I hid out inside our hotel room, lying in bed, crying my eyes out.

*

Our current best research on psychological trauma tells us that recovery from terrorizing life events over which we have no control can be facilitated by revisiting the memories of those events, memories which can be so painful that we have to fight against our instinct to bury them. I discovered this firsthand through my work in therapy. Making room in our minds for the distressing images that we would rather push aside offers us a chance to reexperience the moments of a traumatic experience, giving us the opportunity to have control over our movements and our speech in ways that were denied to us at the time.

We might explain this process by what neuroscientists have characterized as "episodic reconsolidation." The common assumption used to be that once short-term memories had been converted (or consolidated) to long-term memories, they were immune to further manipulation, but this assumption has been challenged in the last decade. Drawing from animal studies, scientists have argued that the process of remembering renders a memory fragile and malleable. Reconsolidation makes the representation stable once again, but there is a gap that opens up there. The hypothesis is that with traumatic memories, we exploit that gap by altering our emotional response to the memory while it is in a malleable state so that it reconsolidates with new emotional information.

All this is to say that while we cannot change what happened to us, we are not powerless about it, either. We have control over the way we live with trauma, over how it metabolizes in our brains and bodies. We have control over how we take care of ourselves, now, by opening ourselves up to the range of emotional and sensorimotor responses that get jammed in a traumatic experience. Talking back, even fighting back, however belatedly, can effect positive neuroplastic changes, which can help bypass the overwhelming feelings of helplessness that otherwise threaten to sink us.

And while this kind of reparative work can be incomparably hard, the alternative is to risk staying permanently stuck. I suspect that this is true not just for survivors of sexual violence but for anyone who has been through a traumatic experience, like those who have seen the horrors of war or suffered a natural disaster. I am convinced that this kind of work can also help to heal the incidents of trauma that are common in childhood, such as unexpected fury at the hand of an angry parent, or the gaping wound of abandonment left by an absent parent.

I feel unburdened, bit by bit, each time I work through the memory of what happened to me in apartment 1070, 142 boulevard Massena. But each time my body betrays me, each time my heart races, I am faced with an awareness of the peculiar, even paradoxical, relationship I have to my own body. Sometimes it can be hard to know which parts of me are authentic—my implacable will, which pushes through, or my injured flesh, which blocks the way? The biological truth of my trauma is anchored in me, but it lives there like a parasite. And as I move in and out of recovery I am reminded that however much work I do, healing from a traumatic experience is never complete. This is one of the most significant facts about psychological trauma. It is permanent. The psychological damage that results from the experience of terrorizing life events over which we have no control is profound. It sticks around for life. It is a chronic condition, which makes recovery from traumatic events an ongoing process. And like any chronic illness, there are flare-ups and times of remission. Sometimes I am taken aback when my anxiety erupts, but PTSD is a stress disorder and my periods of high anxiety usually can be traced directly to the amount of stress that I am under at any given time.

As my work on this book was coming to a close I experienced, for the first time in a long while, a serious flare-up. I spent a good portion of my sabbatical year sequestered in my home office, typing away, writing the first three quarters of this book. I spent parts of the next year, whatever time I could steal away from work commitments, finishing a first draft. For months on end over the course of those two years I was completely immersed in this project, and yet the experience was relatively anxiety-free. The writing had not been triggering; in fact, I had quite enjoyed the process, which had been surprisingly satisfying, not from a therapeutic perspective but from a creative one. During all that time I had not been thinking about much beyond simply getting the book done. More to the point, I had not anticipated how I would feel, handing it off to others. But then I finished my first draft and it was time to show it to my first readers—Bruce, who had already read chunks of it, a few of my closest friends, and my family. And then I started to think about the reality of publishing it — of putting this book out into the world. And then I stopped breathing.

Although I had been "out" as a rape survivor for years, it quickly became clear that it was one thing to tell friends and acquaintances about something that had happened to me a long time ago and quite another to publish a book about it, with all my intimacies in painstaking detail, for anyone to see. And while the adult in me had all these good reasons for writing this book and was ready to make the story public, it wasn't just her story to tell. Buried somewhere inside of me is that young, innocent woman who was last seen scribbling in her journal in the summer of 1990 on a train from Amsterdam to Paris, musing about her summer adventures and the souvenirs that she was planning to buy for her friends and family. If it is anyone's story to tell it is that young woman's, who had her playfulness stolen from her later that night, and here I was, getting ready to expose her, again.

I spent a couple of months struggling to catch a deep breath before I was ready to admit that, once more, I needed some extra help. I decided to go back on a daily dose of clonazepam, at least for a while, until my body calmed down. In the meantime, Anique and I decided that it might be a good idea for me to return to the local trauma resource center. Maybe writing the book had jarred some new memories and maybe I would feel better if I could move around and release the hold that they quite obviously still had over me.

We booked ourselves into one of the soundproof rooms for a few sessions, and there I found myself returning once again to boulevard Massena. We dimmed the lights and I lay on a gym mat, eyes closed, trying to connect with the emotional and somatic memories that were now over twenty years old. At my request, and as usual, Anique sat a few feet away from me. While I needed her in the room with me to help me, to coach me and to help me feel safe, I also needed the distance. Whenever I am doing this sort of work I need to know that there is no chance that we will have any physical contact while I follow my memories back. I half-fear that an accidental touch will trigger me, but mostly I worry that I will inadvertently kick her in the face if she is sitting too close.

During one of these sessions I lay there for some time, on my back, trying to clear my mind of any direction so as to let my body take me where it needed to go. Eventually I was back in the bedroom of Édouard Roditi's Paris apartment, feeling the weight of Robert's sweaty body draped heavily over me, while he raped me vaginally. I had felt that before, not just twenty years ago but in this very room, and it was just as gross this time around. But now I felt something new. I felt the knife scratching, digging into the left side of my neck. I was stuck in this body memory, and I was terrified. I managed to choke out a few words, to tell Anique that the knife was pressing into my neck, hurting me, and she told me in no uncertain terms to push it away. This was something that I had never before tried to do, and my arms felt like lead. But after some gentle prodding I picked them up and bent them at the elbows, cradling with both hands the phantom knife that was pressing into my neck, and then the oddest thing happened. I could not push the knife away. Each time I tried I felt it slicing through my hands. I could almost see my hands cut and bleeding.

I was blown away by the vigor of this image. It was as if the knife was real, and here I was, again powerless against its sharp edges. How could I break free without cutting myself? I could not have, back then, and with this awareness I collapsed into tears. When I finally stopped bawling Anique got up and walked to the corner of the room, picked something up, and came back with two boxing gloves. I put these on and with the thick protection of their cushion I tightened my hands around the blade of the knife and forced it off of my neck, pushing it away, hard, until the threat of it there disappeared.

*

Returning to 142 boulevard Massena was an important step toward deflating the emotional hold that the place had over me for twenty years. And it did not kill me, although the stress of it made for one crummy night. But by midday Sunday I decided that I needed to pull myself out of my bad mood and so I called my mom, as I often do when I am feeling low. Talking to her made me feel better, more grounded, and when I got off the phone I made up with Bruce and decided that it was time to take in some sights. It was a beautiful late August day, sunny and warm, but not too humid. We took our time, wandering around the sublime cobblestone streets of Paris. We worked our way through the Left Bank, stopping for reflection at each memory. We paused outside the busy Café Le Conti, and peeked into the lobby of the Hôtel Saint André des Arts. We walked across the rue Saint André des Arts toward the Seine, and then made our way over the Île de la Cité, past the Hôtel-Dieu and the Palais de Justice. We took some pictures as the sun set and finally ended up in the Marais, where we had drinks and I relaxed, charmed by the exquisite pull of this city for what felt like the first time.

By Monday I was feeling much better and ready to do more investigative work. I had brought with me to Paris the transcripts of the pretrial *indictment* and the trial *judgment*, and between them they contained all the relevant details about the case. My plan was to go to the Palais de Justice to see if I could find out any information about Robert Dinges. In truth, the only thing I really wanted to know was whether or not he had died in jail. I had long wondered if the fact that he was HIV-positive had turned his eight-year sentence into a life sentence, and it felt like time to find out.

*

When I think about the night of August 1, 1990, I think about it as the night that I was raped. I think about the way that Robert rammed his penis into me with rage and indifference to my pain, the way he moved briskly from one penetration to the next without giving me a second to organize my thoughts or a chance to fight back, to protest. I hardly ever think of it as the night that I was almost killed. When my mind wanders in that direction I get this image of myself as a ragdoll, suspended, lifeless in midair, held up by my hair, with someone poking at me, prodding all of my orifices. In these instants my left shoulder folds forward to protect my neck and my anus muscles shut tight. That's me *not* surviving. I picture the kitchen knife carving faint scratches on my breasts and I remember holding my breath, waiting for it to sink in. I think that that was Robert's moment to kill me, and he missed it.

When I replay the events of that night in my mind I wonder why, in the face of Robert's intimidating comments at dinner, did I not run straight out the front door. Why, when I became scared, did I take the time to go to the bathroom to think? I might have been in there for only ten seconds, but it was a costly ten seconds. I do not blame myself for Robert's savage behavior, but I can't help but blame myself for not reading the warning signs better or more quickly. I know that this is not entirely reasonable, and that what seems obvious in retrospect — that Robert was intending to hurt me — is not always or even usually obvious at the time. But the feeling that I made a mistake that night, that I should not have gone to the bathroom but instead headed straight out the front door, has stuck with me. I think a lot about those ten seconds. These thoughts feed into my catastrophic thinking and have impacted my ability to bounce back from making any manner of mistake.

Years ago, in anticipation of starting my new job at the University of Guelph, I bought a brand new car, a shiny silver Toyota Echo. I hadn't had it a month when, on a road trip to Winnipeg, the windshield was chipped by an errant stone on a gravelly highway road. It was a small chip, but I was devastated by it to the point of hysteria. I had a sense that I was seriously overreacting, but still, for days — weeks even — I could not shake the feeling that something horrible had happened to me because of a bad choice that I had made. I am not sure if this could be properly called a mistake, but I was in a situation over which I had some control, and which I could have therefore avoided. Had I been able to see into the future, for instance, I would not have taken my brand new car on a road trip. And had I been able to predict what was going to happen to me on that ill-fated night years before, I would not have gone to the bathroom but instead shot directly out the front door.

Whenever I feel like I have made a mistake I become overwhelmed with feelings of failure and helplessness, and the notion that I am profoundly unlucky pervades my thinking. At times like this my PTSD-related symptoms flare up, and my responses to life's ordinary blunders become disproportionate. My intrusive thoughts intensify, and I have to distract myself from imagining the life of someone I care dearly about being violently cut short. My breathing becomes shallow, a tedious reminder of the hour that I held it, twenty years earlier. I become hyper-vigilant, on guard, as it were, as if this time I am not going to miss any clues. And I have a hard time closing my eyes at night, which means that I end up relying on my favorite, hazardous cocktail of benzos and scotch to help me get to sleep. In these moments of self-soothing the alcohol seems to work. For a time, at least, it helps to change the way I feel; it replaces my anxiety with sensations of pleasure and calm. But in the final analysis, alcohol is a bogus reward system. Although it seems to activate the hormones that regulate stress, it is a form of dysregulation that fails to address the underlying causes of these flare-ups. What I have learned is that I must eventually face them, and when I do my troubling symptoms subside, hastened by the realization that I am caught in a traumatic flashback.

*

Bruce and I spent half a day in the Palais de Justice, getting shuffled around from one office to the next in our quest to find out some information about Robert Dinges. This task was complicated by the fact that most of the people we spoke to were not bilingual, and Bruce's French was not any better than mine. After a time we wound up in the office of the greffe of the Cour d'Assises de Paris, where we found a woman who, although she spoke no English, was able to understand our inquiry and was willing to help us. After studying the documents I had brought along she warned us not to expect much. The case was old. Seventeen years had passed since Robert had been sentenced, and she was skeptical that she would be able to find any information on him. But after some fiddling on her computer she said that she had something for us. According to prison records, Robert had served his complete term of eight years before being released. He had not, therefore, died in jail.

When I heard this information something within me shifted. I am not sure exactly what it was, but the news moved me forward, closer to the ending of the story. It made me feel lighter, and it also made me think about Stream, I guess because he was another missing piece of the puzzle. A few years after I started therapy with Anique I stopped talking to him, and we hadn't had any contact in over ten years. I did not intend to cut him out of my life, but that is what I did. We had stayed in touch over the years following the rape, and I would occasionally visit him in New York City, where he had returned to live after graduating from Bard College. Over time I had managed to move past my anger toward him. I no longer blamed him for what had happened, but there was simply no way to erase his integral role in the events of August 1. That left a horrible stain on him, an unfair burden that he did not deserve and that he would have to carry around for the rest of his life, and it marked me as well. It took me a long while to understand it, but I used to feel really off after our phone calls. What I finally realized was that talking to Stream made me feel dirty. Contact with him triggered my internalized feelings of shame and disgust. I felt gross about myself whenever we spoke. It was not his fault, but I could not find any way around it. So, eventually, I just stopped talking to him.

I feel a lot of compassion for him now, and I especially feel tenderness for that young lover of mine, who, on a warm August night in the most fabled city in the world, following his first ever adventure-filled summer in Europe, hurried back to boulevard Massena after missing out on a dinner date with his mentor, keen to reunite with the then love of his life, oblivious as to what was waiting for him there. Now I missed him; I wondered where he was and how he was doing.

Bruce and I continued to wander around the building for a while and eventually ended up in another office where the main clerk spoke fluent English. She did some further checking around on our behalf before confirming what we had just learned. Robert had lived to serve his complete sentence of eight years in jail. If he had died after his release, she told us, she would have no record of it, but we could find this out by writing to the town hall of his hometown of Betwiller, Bas-Rhin. She said that they would have a death certificate on hand of anyone who had been born there, regardless of where they had died. We thanked this woman for her help and called it a day.

*

The story of my rape and the events both preceding and following it contains no falsehoods, so far as I know. I have double-checked the facts against my rape file and relevant journal entries, and I ran the final product by my best fact-checker, my dad. But there may be some crucial feature of the story that never made it into this account, because I alone was witness to it and the memory of it is something to which I have no conscious access. If traumatic memories are convoluted, rendering certain aspects of a traumatic experience ineradicable and obliterating others, then it should come as no surprise if autobiographical stories about traumatic experiences are incomplete.

A story like mine is necessarily partial, not only because of the nature and reliability of traumatic memories, but because while truth is a matter of fact, it is also a matter of perspective. Which facts stand out in our memories and which details seem to us significant depend on which truths matters to us. That does not mean that there is no fact of the matter about what happened in Édouard Roditi's Paris apartment on August 1, 1990, but it does mean that there is not just one correct way of representing the events of that night. How we tell a story, which parts we choose to emphasize and which parts we leave out, is a reflection of our unconscious biases as well as our interests, that is, what we care about. Truth is a matter of interpretation; it is partial and subject to perspective.

You can illustrate a map to show topography or population numbers, depending on whether your interest in an area is physical, or, say, political. Both would be accurate maps, but both partial representations. And sometimes, like in the case of the London Underground map, geography might be forsaken (for instance, the tube lines and the River Thames are smoothed out) in order to highlight topological features (like the relative positions of stations along the lines). Although there is a distortion here, the precise physical locations of the stations are irrelevant to most travelers, as Harry Beck, the acclaimed designer of the first diagrammatic map of the London Tube, realized.

In addition to the details of my experience that never made it on to these pages because they are lost to memory, it is part of the nature of storytelling to embellish and omit for emphasis. When we recount our own tales we focus on the features that to us loom large and omit the ones that to us seem irrelevant. Studies show that it is likely that we do this early on, when we first give linguistic shape to our narrative, such that over time we don't even see ourselves as exaggerating or minimizing. Again, this is not to say that there is no fact of the matter about what happened to me on the night of August 1, 1990, but rather that there are a lot of facts and no objective way, no one correct way, of picking out which facts are salient. The story as I have told it might vary in detail, though likely not in substance, from the story that Stream would tell, or Roditi, if he were alive, or the police, or even Robert Dinges. And while it is a true story, from start to finish, it is in the end the story as I remember it.

*

I spent less than five minutes considering whether to pursue further the matter of whether Robert had died after being released from jail. For years I had wondered if he had survived his jail term, but our morning at the Palais de Justice had answered that question, and for some reason it just didn't matter to me whether or for how long he had lived beyond that. That said, I occasionally wonder about him. If he is still alive, what kind of a person is he now? He must have been deeply troubled back in 1990. I take his violent behavior toward me as evidence of that, not to mention his previous prison record and his alcohol and drug abuse.

I sometimes speculate about why he entered a guilty plea. Was it simply that the evidence against him, from the semen specimen to the knife, ruled out any other alternative? Was this a strategic move that he made on the counsel of his lawyer? Or was it that he felt some remorse for what he had done to me and wanted to take responsibility for it? I know this last explanation is not very likely, but I like to leave it open as a possibility because it permits me to see a grain of decency in Robert. I don't doubt that he had an abusive childhood, as his lawyer described in detail during the sentencing trial, and certainly that would have left him feeling powerless. It is possible that having absolute power over me eliminated those unwanted feelings in him, if only temporarily. If I focus on his past, or, rather, on my hypothetical reconstruction of it, then I am able to feel compassion for him. Not a lot, but some.

I also wonder about the extent to which he had control over his actions that night. Freedom is a thorny concept, but there is a relatively straightforward meaning of the term that we use when we want to distinguish between authoritarian states and democratic ones. This sense of freedom picks up on the notion of individual autonomy, of being able to manage one's own affairs and raises the question about the degree to which the state has a right to interfere with the decisions of its citizens on how they should live their lives. While most everyone agrees that there are important limits to our freedom, especially when our actions infringe on the rights of others (so, for example, hate crime laws place relatively noncontroversial limits on freedom of speech), there is disagreement over where to draw this line. This matter is complicated by the fact of value pluralism, that is, the patent, widespread difference of opinion over what makes a good life good. Is it climbing Mount Everest, or making art? Is it having children, or going to church? Is it political activism, or obedience to the state, or having the right to marry a person of your own sex? In an authoritarian state the government tends to decide on behalf of its citizens what sorts of things they should value, and why. A key feature of a liberal democratic society, on the other hand, is its acceptance of value pluralism and its willingness to let its citizens engage in those pursuits which they deem valuable, to tailor-make their own versions of the good life.

Freedom from an interfering state is, arguably, a necessary condition for individual autonomy. If the state is too meddling, then our ability to manage our own affairs as we see fit will be restricted by the state's authority over us. But freedom from an interfering state is no guarantee of individual autonomy; something more is needed for that. Genuine autonomy demands that we act deliberately, that our beliefs, values, and decisions are really are own, and this means that we need to have a handle on the reasons that shape our behavior. But this is no easy task. Our reasons for acting are not always transparent, even to us. Self-knowledge is not a given, but it is not out of reach, either. It is something that we can work at, and with understanding comes options. Knowing why we behave the way we do can help us to see choices where we previously saw none.

I am no model of autonomous living, having had the experience of being raped shape most of my major life decisions for well over a decade of my life. But since starting in therapy I have come to see some of the ways in which the rape has unconsciously influenced my behavior over the years. Here is a trivial but tangible example of this. For many years following the rape I slept on my stomach with my head cranked left and my left arm tight to my side, folded in half, with my fist balled up in the crook of my neck. I had been sleeping on my stomach since I was a kid, but it was only after the rape that my head turned to favor my left side exclusively, though if you had pointed this out to me in the years following the rape it would have come as a surprise. I had adopted this protective stance without knowing it, and it was only after I started my work in therapy that I became aware of it, and when I did it was a startling revelation. I was taken aback by just how subliminal the impact of trauma could be.

Once I became aware of the way the trauma had been controlling my body I was able to make a choice about it, to loosen my fist and, should I wish, turn my head to the right. What had been involuntary became optional.

Having some understanding of the reasons for our behavior improves our odds of seeing choices where we
previously saw none, thereby giving us the opportunity
to act deliberately rather than acting from historical, un-
processed emotional and somatic states. Screening the
left side of my neck from harm is a trivial case of this,
but failing to look inward at the causes of our behavior
can have dire repercussions, like when someone who
was abused as a child becomes an abuser himself. There
may be something automatic about this transition, the
move from victim to aggressor, unconsciously adopted
by the victim as a way of erasing the emotionally intolerable feelings of vulnerability that are so often the result of
an abusive childhood. But this development is not inevi-
table, of course, since not everyone who suffers an abusive childhood turns into an abuser, and at least one way
to avoid it is to face our demons head on and get some
control over them, instead of letting them control us.

I am unaware of the extent to which Robert was
capable of self-restraint in the summer of 1990; I don't
know how seriously he battled his demons or how aware
he was of his own violent tendencies. But I am sure that,
on the night that he changed my life forever, he was quite
unable to keep his impulses in check and put a stop to
his violent behavior, which makes me think that I was
lucky to have gotten out alive. But while Robert might
have been out of control when he raped me he is not,
therefore, beyond reproach. In part, our culpability lies
in our choice to deal with the challenging issues that
dominate our lives, though certainly not everyone has
the time, resources or inclination to hire a therapist to
help facilitate the process — that was my method, and it

is a particularly white, middle-class, Western approach to self-knowledge. But however we get there, genuine autonomy demands that we act deliberately, that our beliefs, values, and decisions are our own. I am certain that this kind of self-awareness can be gained through a myriad of different ways, including traditional methods of self-reflection like meditation and therapy, and also nontraditional ones like writing, doing yoga, dancing, playing a sport, listening to music, or making art, to name just a few possibilities.

As this suggests, freedom from an interfering government is not the only barrier to genuine autonomy. The right to reflect is not universal. It is a privilege afforded to those of us in affluent societies who have time to spare, and who are not otherwise burdened by fundamental problems, like poverty, malnutrition or ill health, problems that, at least in male-dominated societies, women suffer disproportionately. Add to this women's lack of equality under the law in those same societies, as well as their lack of equal access to education and basic social institutions of welfare, and it becomes clear that it is not just women's bodies but their basic human rights that are under attack in male-dominated societies. If we needed evidence of this, no better case has been made for the dearth of gender equality in the developing world than that put forth by Pulitzer Prize winners Nicholas D. Kristof and Sheryl WuDunn in their inspiring new book *Half the Sky*, both an unblinking account of women's oppression worldwide and a moving and passionate call to arms. And while men stand to benefit from the structural inequalities found in cultures of male domination, it is clear that they too pay a high price for this privilege in terms of the social pressure on them to live up to masculine ideals of stoicism and emotional repression. Barriers to equality and autonomy are rooted in long-standing attitudes and traditions not only about women but also about men and our respective roles in society.

*

Bruce and I spent the rest of the week in Paris bumming around, acting like tourists. Once I had finished my business at the Palais de Justice I was ready for some sightseeing, but there was more to it than that. I wanted to be able to experience the Paris of movies and books, the one that is in the collective imagination, and not the Paris of boulevard Massena. I wanted to get lost in the wonder and romance of this magnificent city like other people did. I wanted to fill my mind with new images of Paris.

Bruce and I went to the Musée d'Orsay, the Musée Rodin, and the Centre Pompidou. We wandered around the Louvre, chilled out in the Jardin du Luxembourg, and stood underneath the Eiffel Tower, looking up. We went back to the Marais and explored the old Jewish quarter. We ate in charming restaurants, did some shopping, and spent too much money. Over the course of a few days my body calmed down, and by the end of the week I was truly relaxed, and I decided it was time to let Bruce inch his way back close to me. I thought it might be a good idea to have the image of someone I loved lying on top of my naked body in the City of Light.

*

Over the course of the last ten years I have come out as a rape survivor to friends, family, colleagues, students, and strangers. At times I have done so for political reasons, but my initial motivation was personal. The double life I had been leading up to that point had become unsustainable. The disconnect between my relatively high-functioning public persona and the emotional cacophony of my inner life was too much to bear. I needed to reconcile the disparate parts of my identity, but to do so I first needed to face the shame and anger that had been festering inside of me for years. The degree of self-preoccupation required for this was colossal.

And still, challenges remain. Because trauma is a chronic condition, healing happens in fits and starts. And sometimes, just when I think I have turned a corner with respect to my recovery, I am beleaguered by the images in my head which do not belong there, images which can be so loud that I still find it hard to believe that they are invisible to others. It is now over twenty years since I was raped, and although these images have quieted down, they have not gone away. They haunt me most during stressful periods in my life, but they stick around even when I am not having a flare-up and remain easily provoked by signs of dissonance in my life. When Bruce is late on his cycle home from work, I have visions of his body mangled underneath a streetcar. When I am watching my niece or nephew splash around a pool on a peaceful, sunny summer day, I can't help but imagine one of them hitting their head on an unforgiving concrete edge. And when a member of my family is unexpectedly unreachable by phone, I become convinced that someone has suffered a gruesome accident. Catastrophe is always the first place I go.

I have come to accept that these intrusive thoughts

and the images that come bundled up with them are mine for life, but like any chronic disease alongside the flare-ups there are periods of remission, times when I feel unencumbered. The human condition is fragile, and human experience can be brutal. It is important to steal moments of grace where we find them and delight in them. I am able to feel joy and pleasure, and in increments I feel free. I have by any measure a good life, and I am truly grateful for this. But I will never have the easy, carefree bond with my body in sexual relationships that I envy in others.

I was reminded of this a few years back, when Bruce and I attended a book launch for the publication of a "field guide" for men who want to make their women happy in bed. The book is clever and irreverent. It is brimming with useful nuggets on how to arouse the anatomical wonders of women. The tone is breezy and erotic—raunchy, even—without ever being crude. The launch was at a local bar and Bruce and I found ourselves squeezed in amongst a crowd of scenesters, everyone clambering to hear (and see) the smart and sexy writer talk about her smart and sexy book. The entertaining and suggestive discussion that ensued between the author and her interviewer had everyone in the room rapt; it hit all the right notes with the urban, sophisticated audience.

I can talk about G-spots and orgasms as openly as the next person, and I laughed along with the rest of the crowd as the author euphemistically addressed the "bush pilots" in the room. But there was something stilted to my laughter, not quite false but not entirely honest, either. Because no matter how much erotica I consume or how evolved my discussions with friends about sex may be, I will never possess the insouciant attitude to lovemaking that I envy in others. Sex is not always a challenge for me, and there are times when I sail through the act of making love uninterrupted. But there are times, more often than not, when it is not so easy. These days I am able to see humor in this, thankfully, and Bruce and I will share a good laugh about my inhibitions as we lay together in bed with the lights on while he follows my instructions to not touch me here, or there, or even there. I covet the carefree, uninhibited way in which some women get to play around with their bodies. I will never have that, but my years of forced attention on my body and its held trauma have brought me something else—an awareness of my own needs and a willingness to take care of them. And that, I am certain, is worth something.

I had this thought as I was listening to the author talk about getting lucky. This was the fall of 2010, and I had just finished the first draft of this book, and the juxtaposition between the two books made me smile inwardly, and then I had a look around. There must have been a couple of hundred people in the room, and probably half of them were women. I speculated about the odds; who in the audience might stand to benefit from reading the book that we were there to celebrate, and who might stand to benefit from reading one like mine? How many women in this room, I wondered, are holding their breath right now? How many are feeling unhinged?

*

Coming out as a rape survivor helped me to integrate my inner turmoil and public persona, because it allowed me to show myself without disguise. Representing myself honestly and having others bear witness has left me with a feeling of justice, understood in the broadest sense of being treated well. Being treated well, by both individuals and social institutions, requires that our experiences in life be recognized and reflected back to us. Sharing our life stories with the people that we care about, stories of joy but also of horror, gives others an opportunity to attest to our experiences and allows us to flesh out the human connections in our communities which are central to us.

As rape survivors, talking about our traumatic experiences can help make whole our personal identities and therefore can play an important role in the healing process. But there are also decisive political reasons for being outspoken. Talking about rape can help us to see it as a problem that is the result of the way that societies are structured and resources and power distributed. The fact that rape is a social problem can be hard to remember, because rape is also intensely personal and deeply isolating; it is a violation that is typically experienced in private, held as a secret, and buried in our bodies and in our sexuality in ways that can make us think we are alone in the experience. But despite the formidable personal challenges that survivors face, the widespread systematic debasing of women's and children's bodies by men is a problem that extends beyond victims of violence in the same way that poverty is a problem that reaches beyond individual poor people, which is why providing food for one hungry family or putting one rapist in jail is only a Band-Aid solution. As feminists have been arguing for decades, while violence against women may take different forms and range in severity, it persists as part of a system of oppression and gender discrimination that is rooted in structural inequalities between men and women.

We face a formidable challenge, and the social, economic, political, and educational changes that are needed to bring about social justice therefore requires political will of the strongest order, exercised not only by governments but also by citizens, including those who stand to lose privileges as a result. Sexual violence happens to individuals, to be sure; it is what happened to me, to my friend's friend, to some of my students, and to the women and young girls I met in Botswana. But if we are concerned with putting an end to it, we need to approach the problem of sexual violence through the framework of the age-old patriarchal structure of societies.

*

It has taken me a long time to shake the feeling of being unlucky. In the years following my second HIV test I grew skeptical of the negative test result. I had been tested ten months after the rape, but I knew that in extremely rare cases it could take up to twelve months to show a positive result, and while the odds of this were infinitesimal I began to suspect that I was the one in a million. I knew that I was being completely irrational, but this was yet another case where I could not talk myself out of the catastrophic thinking that is so typical among trauma survivors. But a couple of years after I started in therapy I felt ready to let go of my irrational thinking, or, at least, to put it to a test, so I scheduled myself for a third HIV test. This time the wait between taking the test and getting the result was shorter, and easier, and when I was told that I was HIV-negative I actually believed it.

I used to feel ashamed of my bad luck when bad things would happen to me. Like getting that chip in my car window, it felt like part of a pattern of badness, like a rut out of which I would never be able to claw my way. I don't feel that way anymore. The work that I have done in therapy has allowed me to move beyond the place of trauma that dominated my life for so many years. I may revisit it in body and in mind, but I am no longer stuck there. I can now step out of my situation and see it from the outside, and from this perspective I look pretty darn lucky. I had one bad thing happen to me, but I am well aware of my good fortune that it was just that one. And I am lucky that throughout my recovery I have had a tremendous support system, with devoted and loving parents and sisters, smart and compassionate friends, and an extraordinary therapist. I have had the privilege of being raised in a family that espoused liberal and progressive values, with a focus on education and social justice, and with the intellectual and financial resources to back me through the various stages of my recovery. I am lucky to have been able to find a community of like-minded people to share my life with—my friends, my true oasis. And I am incredibly fortunate to have been born in Canada and thus to have open to me opportunities in life, in play and in work, that are simply not available to women in other parts of the world. And I am also, now, lucky in love.

*

For close to twenty years, August 1 had been the only anniversary in my life that had any meaning to me. The date haunted me each year; in the weeks leading up to it, I was always more apt than usual to be triggered. Even in the first decade following the rape, when I had very little conscious appreciation of the impact of the trauma on my inner life, my body remembered the significance of the date and put me through a trial of typical PTSD-related symptoms. In later years, once I started in therapy, I tried to combat the oppressiveness of this date through various techniques. Once, for example, I bought Anique a bunch of gifts and gave them to her on August 1. Another time I spent the day treating myself to spa services and expensive meals. But still, my summers were marked by the time before, and after.

I expected this pattern to be life-long, but six years ago Bruce and I bought a house together and, in a glitter of remarkable coincidence, the possession date was August 1. For a long time the idea of a stable relationship and a permanent home were unimaginable to me. And now, here I was, buying a house with my life partner and taking claim to it on the date that, for over twenty years, left me unable to take a deep breath. August 1 used to mean something else to me—Robert, boulevard Massena, Stream, Roditi—but not anymore. I was handed an opportunity to reinvent the meaning of that date, and I was not about to pass it up. It would be a stretch to say that August 1 is now a date I celebrate, but it is no longer a date I dread. It is instead a date that marks more than just one transformation in my life.

*

Acknowledgments

If writing is a solitary experience, the process of making a book like this one is anything but, and I could not have pulled it off on my own. I am indebted to many people, and I want to start by thanking those individuals whose work has been integral to helping me develop some of the main ideas in this book.

Over the last fifty years we have seen a wealth of feminist scholarship thrive in a diverse array of fields, challenging our traditional conceptions of everything from art and politics to race and history. I have been deeply influenced and inspired by feminist thought and activism—liberal and radical, first-wave to post-punk—in books and music and film, organized and on the streets. This work has thoroughly shaped the way that I see the world, and in particular the way that I think about rape and violence against women, to such an extent that I can no longer distinguish where it ends and my own thought begins. It has also given me great personal and intellectual sustenance, bolstering my philosophical outlook and worldview. I owe a considerable debt to these revolutionary individuals, the women and men who through theory and practice have broadened our understanding of gender inequality and its impact on well-functioning societies.

I have also benefited tremendously from the scholarly work on psychological trauma, an area of study that has exploded over the last few decades and now goes by its own disciplinary moniker, "trauma studies." Trauma studies crisscrosses the humanities, social sciences, and natural sciences and spans a broad range of fields, including philosophy, history, literary theory, psychology, feminist theory, anthropology, psychiatry, neurobiology, and neurochemistry. I have sifted through this research and my hope is that this book reflects the main ideas currently circulating in the discipline. I have tried to present this material in straightforward terms and without the use of technical jargon, wherever possible, so as not to distract the reader from the story I wished to tell. If this effort has resulted in any inaccuracies the fault of that is, of course, mine alone. Please see the following "further reading" section for a selection of recent and influential research in trauma studies.

This book got its legs during my sabbatical from the University of Guelph in 2008–2009, and I am grateful to the university for providing me with an open intellectual environment in which to pursue this work. It was during that sabbatical that I traveled to Maun, Botswana, to work at Women Against Rape (WAR), with the support of the University of Guelph in partnership with Uniterra, and I want to thank both organizations for the opportunity to participate in Uniterra's innovative volunteer initiative, Leave for Change. My time in Maun was pivotal in helping me think through some of the key themes in this book, and the people I met there had a profound impact on me. I am particularly indebted to the staff at WAR, and especially to my good friend, Rebecca Navoo Hengari.

My colleagues and friends in the Department of Philosophy at the University of Guelph have shown interest and enthusiasm for this book. I am fortunate for their support, and I am particularly thankful to Andrew Bailey and Patricia Sheridan, who read earlier drafts of this work with an eye for detail that is a mark of a good philosopher. I also want to thank Mark Fenske, a cognitive neuroscientist (and author of *The Winner's Brain*) in the Department of Psychology at the University of Guelph, who generously looked over my claims about the science of the brain with expert eyes.

It is hard to get any book published nowadays, let alone a book on rape, but I caught a glimmer of that possibility when Charlotte Sheedy, literary agent extraordinaire, took me on. Charlotte instantly saw the value in this book and her resolve gave me the early boost I needed. I am very grateful to her and to her associate, Mackenzie Brady. I want to thank David Brent at the University of Chicago Press, another individual who quickly understood what I was trying to accomplish here. Thanks also to Priya Nelson and all the people at the University of Chicago Press who helped me bring this book into publishable form. And thanks to everyone at Freehand Books, my Canadian publisher, and in particular Kelsey Attard.

I owe a great debt to Anique Rosenbaum—anyone who has read this book can see that. Anique brought me out of a dark place, and she continues to guide me, mind and body. I am sure that the world is full of great therapists, but I am equally sure that, with Anique, I lucked out. My heart is full up with appreciation and respect for her.

There have been many people in my life who have supported this project and who have offered help and advice. I am thankful to them all, but I want to single out Bruce Lynn, Rachel Gorenstein, Josh Greenhut, and Susan Rich—my first and closest readers. And an extra thanks goes to Susan for steering me through every stage. These friends of mine are without equal.

Bruce, of course, is much more than a friend, and his support for me, in all that I do, never wavers. I am forever lucky for that.

August 1, 1990, was a bad night not just for me but also for my parents, Martin and Roxy. Yet, from the moment that my mom met me in Toronto to take me home on August 2, they have held me up. Their strength on my behalf fueled my own commitment to recovery, and their abiding love has been the backdrop for all of my endeavors, this book included. I can always count on them, and on my sisters, Jacqueline and Lisa, who are a constant source of support and friendship. They are exceptional women of charm and brilliance and I look up to them both. And special thanks go to my amazingly talented nephew and niece, Ethan and Talia. The unmitigated joy they bring to my life makes anything seem possible.

We are a tight crew, my family, and they have been by my side as I conceived of this book, immersed myself in the writing, and sought to bring it into the world. Its publication signals a turning point in the story of my rape, not just for me but also for my parents and sisters. A close family like ours means that we rejoice in each other's achievements, but also that we suffer each other's misfortunes. What happened to me was terribly hard on each of them, but bringing this story into the world is a happy outcome for us all. It may be impossible to thank them sufficiently for their support over the years, but I will sure continue to try.

Further Reading

The field of trauma studies may be only a few decades old but the current research is advancing at a breakneck pace. The volume of publications coming out of diverse areas within the humanities, social sciences, and natural sciences is vast, and the upshot of all this good work is that we are getting an increasingly clear picture of the causes and effects of traumatic life events and the processes of recovery from them. What follows is a selection of the influential work that has shaped this field over the last few decades.

One of the leading figures in trauma studies is Bessel A. van der Kolk, an outspoken proponent of body-based, or somatic, therapies who helped to define the current paradigm for understanding psychological trauma through neurobiology. Over the last thirty years van der Kolk has authored and coauthored countless articles in the field, but a good place to start would be with the essays collected in *Traumatic Stress: The Effects of Overwhelming Experience on the Mind, Body, and Society* (New York: Guilford Press, 1996), which he coedited with Alexander C. McFarlane and Lars Weisaeth. This important volume contains a number of articles by van der Kolk, including his well-known "The Body Keeps the Score" (1994) and his coauthored article with Onno van der Hart and Charles R. Marmar on Janet and dissociation, "Dissociation and Information Processing in Posttraumatic

Stress Disorder." Judith Lewis Herman is another key figure in the field, and her groundbreaking *Trauma and Recovery: The Aftermath of Violence—From Domestic Abuse to Political Terror* (New York: Basic Books, 1992), which helped to solidify the connection between violence against women and PTSD, has become a landmark work in the field. Also influential has been Cathy Caruth's work, including *Unclaimed Experience: Trauma, Narrative, and History* (Baltimore, MD: Johns Hopkins University Press, 1996), and her collected volume of essays, *Trauma: Explorations in Memory* (Baltimore, MD: Johns Hopkins University Press, 1995), which contains contributions from artists, sociologists, anthropologists, and psychiatrists. Ian Hacking's *Rewriting the Soul: Multiple Personality and the Sciences of Memory* (Princeton, NJ: Princeton University Press, 1995) has helped to frame our current conceptions of trauma and memory. His work on looping effects can be found here and also in his *The Social Construction of What?* (Cambridge, MA: Harvard University Press, 1999).

The story of how PTSD made it into the *DSM III* is compellingly told by Wilbur J. Scott in his definitive study, "PTSD in DSM-III: A Case in the Politics of Diagnosis and Disease," *Social Problems* 37, no. 3 (1990): 294–310, and by Allan Young in his *The Harmony of Illusions: Inventing Post-Traumatic Stress Disorder* (Princeton, NJ: Princeton University Press, 1995). The early history of trauma in Europe and America, from the beginnings of the psychologization of the concept and Erichsen's "railway spine" through Charcot's "traumatic hysteria" and the shell shock epidemic of the First World War, is well documented in a superb collection of historical essays edited by Paul Lerner and Mark Micale, *Traumatic Pasts: History, Psychiatry, and Trauma in the Modern Age, 1870–1930* (Cambridge: Cambridge University Press, 2001). Ruth Leys's *Trauma: A Genealogy* (Chicago: University of Chicago Press, 2000) provides yet another perspective on

the history and development of the concept of psychological trauma, and Jeffrey Masson's controversial theory about
Freud and his seduction theory can be found in his *The Assault on Truth: Freud's Suppression of the Seduction Theory*
(New York: Penguin, 1984).

Because the *DSM* is more than a diagnostic tool—because
it is a book that has the power to change lives—it has at-
tracted its fair share of criticism over the years, but the fire-
storm of controversy over the recently published *DSM 5*,
largely from within its own ranks, is like nothing we have
seen before. Allen Frances, who was the chair of the *DSM IV*
Task Force and is an outspoken critic of the new revision, dis-
cusses many of the issues which have generated criticism in a
series of blog posts available at http://www.psychologytoday
.com/blog/dsm5-in-distress. Serious worries about the medi-
calization of everyday distress and of the validity of PTSD
as a sound diagnostic category have been eloquently ex-
pressed by Derek Summerfield in his "The Invention of Post-
Traumatic Stress Disorder and the Social Usefulness of a Psychiatric Category," *British Medical Journal* 322 (2001): 95–98.
Jerome C. Wakefield's work on the concept of mental disorders and on the construction of diagnostic categories in
the *DSM* has also been influential. His article, coauthored
with Robert L. Spitzer (one of the architects of *DSM III*) and
Allan V. Horwitz, critically examines the ongoing expansion
of the diagnostic criteria for PTSD; see their "Saving PTSD
from Itself in *DSM-V*," *Journal of Anxiety Disorders* 21, no. 2
(2007): 233–41.

The volume of recent scientific work on neuroplasticity is
massive, but for a great nontechnical introduction to the field
I recommend Norman Doidge's bestselling *The Brain That
Changes Itself* (New York: Penguin, 2007). Ruth Lanius has
published important work on the neurobiology of trauma,
and so has Rachel Yehuda; see, for instance, Paul A. Frewen

and Ruth A. Lanius, "Towards a Psychobiology of Posttrau-matic Self-Dysregulation: Reexperiencing, Hyperarousal, Dissociation, and Emotional Numbing," *Annals of the New York Academy of Sciences* 1071 (2006): 110–24; and Rachel Yehuda and Joseph LeDoux, "Response Variation following Trauma: A Translational Neuroscience Approach to Under-standing PTSD," *Neuron* 56, no. 1 (2007): 19–32. There have been a number of recent scientific studies on the *COMT* gene, and these interesting results are discussed in Po Bron-son and Ashley Merryman's "Why Can Some Kids Handle Pressure While Others Fall Apart?" article in *New York Times Sunday Magazine*, February 6, 2013 (http://www.nytimes .com/2013/02/10/magazine/why-can-some-kids-handle -pressure-while-others-fall-apart.html?pagewanted=all & _r=0).

The current science of trauma provides a foundation for the emphasis on somatic therapies as treatment for PTSD. This connection is made explicit in Stephen W. Porges's polyvagal theory, which offers a neurophysiological basis for a brain–body approach to healing from trauma; see his *The Polyvagal Theory: Neurophysiological Foundations of Emo-tions, Attachment, Communication, Self-Regulation* (New York: W. W. Norton, 2011). The clinical turn to somatic ther-apy, on its own or in conjunction with traditional talk ther-apy, has resulted in a number of different treatment ap-proaches by key figures in trauma studies. See, for instance, Babette Rothschild's *The Body Remembers: The Psychophysi-ology of Trauma and Trauma Treatment* (New York: W. W. Norton, 2000); Pat Ogden, Kekuni Minton, and Clare Pain's *Trauma and the Body: A Sensorimotor Approach to Psycho-therapy* (New York: W. W. Norton, 2006); and Peter A. Levine's *In An Unspoken Voice* (Berkeley, CA: North Atlan-tic Books, 2010). Another approach that connects mind and body is EMDR; see Francine Shapiro and Margot Silk Forrest's *EMDR: Eye Movement Desensitization and Reprocessing* (New York: Basic Books, 2004). For an alternative clinical approach, see Edna Foa's therapist guide *Prolonged Exposure Therapy for PTSD: Emotional Processing of Traumatic Experiences* (New York: Oxford, 2007), with Elizabeth A. Hembree and Barbara Olasov Rothbaum.